THE MORAL MEDIA

How Journalists Reason
About Ethics

LEA'S COM0MUNICATION SERIES
Jennings Bryant / Dolf Zillmann, General Editors

For a complete list of titles in LEA's Communication Series, please contact Lawrence Erlbaum Associates, Publishers, at www.erlbaum.com

THE MORAL MEDIA

How Journalists Reason About Ethics

Lee Wilkins
University of Missouri

Renita Coleman
Louisiana State University

LEA

LAWRENCE ERLBAUM ASSOCIATES, PUBLISHERS
2005   Mahwah, New Jersey   London

Lawrence Erlbaum Associates, Inc., Publishers
10 Industrial Avenue
Mahwah, New Jersey 07430

Cover design by Kathryn Houghtaling Lacey

Library of Congress Cataloging-in-Publication Data

Wilkins, Lee.
The moral media : how journalists reason about ethics / Lee Wilkins, Renita Coleman.
    p. cm. — (LEA's communication series)

    Includes bibliographical references and index.
ISBN 0-8058-4474-0 (cloth : alk. paper)
ISBN 0-8058-4475-9 (pbk. : alk. paper)
1. Journalistic ethics. I. Coleman, Renita. II. Title. III. Series.
PN4756.W56   2005
174'.90704—dc22   2004050053
                                                CIP

Books published by Lawrence Erlbaum Associates are printed on acid-free paper, and their bindings are chosen for strength and durability.

Printed in the United States of America
10 9 8 7 6 5 4 3 2 1

To David and John

…and to all the professionals who so generously took time out of their busy day to cooperate with a couple of "ivory tower" academics on a rather long survey

Contents

PART II: THE STRUGGLE TO THINK
DEEPLY—PICTURES, DECEPTION, AND PERSUASION

Preface

This book is designed to provide readers with some preliminary answers to questions about ethical thinking in a professional environment. For those who are or aspire to be journalists, it attempts to describe how some of your professional colleagues make ethical decisions—what is important to them and what influences their thinking. For scholars in journalism and mass communication, it provides some rigorous and empirically grounded answers to questions such as: Do journalists, although they may lack the vocabulary of moral philosophy, reason through moral questions in ways that classical philosophers would recognize? For psychologists, particularly those interested in human development and behavior, it asks if visual information—the kind contained in photographs—aids thinking. And for philosophers who read this book, we attempt to describe how people build their own philosophical worlds, and how those mental constructions actually influence professional practice. What we seek to create is a theoretical loom that weaves the threads of professional life into a recognizable pattern. That's what we hope professionals will find in this book—real lives and real choices they recognize.

We also leave some important questions incompletely explored. This volume, based of necessity in one particular understanding of moral development, cannot fully explore all the alternate explanations to moral development now current in the psychological literature. However, alternative explanations are offered, particularly when they provide additional explanatory power and depth. Furthermore, this book explores only a few of the ethical issues that journalists face. Finally, if people come to this book seeking to learn why people say one thing and do another—particularly when ethics is involved—this volume, although it addresses the question in some ways, will be incomplete. Instead, we hope this work will serve as a beginning on which other scholars, and indeed professionals who are concerned with quality of ethical decision making in the media, can build. We intend this book as a first step—not the last. We invite others to follow.

So, what did we do? First, we asked working professionals to take an ethics test. This paper-and-pencil test, what psychologists call an *instrument*, was devised almost 30 years ago by psychologist James Rest, who was working with nursing students at the University of Minnesota. Rest took the best known of the moral development theories at the time, the work of Harvard psychologist Lawrence Kohlberg, and turned Kohlberg's in-depth interview approach into a "test" that could be completed in less than 1 hour. That test is now known as the *Defining Issues Test* (DIT). It has been given to literally thousands of professionals. This book represents the first publication of journalists' and advertising practitioners' response to the DIT; it compares thinking about ethics by these two groups with the thinking of other professionals.

Part I of the book, therefore, includes chapters that explain the DIT and place it within the larger history of three fields: psychology, philosophy, and mass communication. Part I also includes both a statistical (quantitative) and narrative (qualitative) analysis of journalists' responses to the DIT. Part I represents the baseline scholarship of this volume.

Part II attempts to add to scholarship and theory building in these three disciplines, first through making changes in the DIT that added an element of visual information processing to the test. The impact of visual information on ethical thinking is further tested when race is made a prominent component of that visual information. In addition to pushing the theoretical boundaries of moral development, we attempted, with the help of two colleagues, to think deeply about two issues in applied ethics: deception and persuasion. Members of Investigative Reporters and Editors, arguably the journalism profession's most prestigious professional organization and a group whose ethical decision making has been examined using the case study approach, were surveyed and then interviewed in depth about deception as professionals understand it. The results of that work present both some fine-grained thinking about this issue and a cogent analysis of the external influences that may—and we do believe do—impinge on ethical thinking. Part II concludes with a chapter that reports how advertising professionals respond to the DIT and, in particular, the impact that "client-centered" thinking has on those decisions.

The final section of the book, Part III, explores the larger meaning of this effort and links the results to both theory and practice in philosophy, psychology, and mass communication. We acknowledge that there may be alternate interpretations to our work. However, the concluding portion of the book represents our attempt to make the best case for the melding of theory, practice, and aspiration that this research represents.

In our view, this is a book about connections—among various intellectual disciplines, between the academy and the profession of journalism, and among those of us who believe that what journalists do is essential and that we need to find ways to do it better. We hope the work speaks to multiple audiences, that it makes everyone think, and that it provides a sound base on which to build.

—*Lee Wilkins*
—*Renita Coleman*

Part I

UNDERSTANDING JOURNALISTS' RESPONSES TO MORAL QUESTIONS

CHAPTER 1

Moral Development Theory: A Historical Approach

ITS BEGINNINGS AND ITS LINK TO MORAL PHILOSOPHY

The concept of moral development is a 20th-century notion, although it has strong roots in classical philosophy. Aristotle believed that ethical actions sprang from the character of the actor, and that character was the totality of the expression of the cardinal Greek virtues. Aristotle did not consider that character was developed so much as it was exercised by daily living. The person who exercised his or her character in an ethical way was called a *phrenemos*: Greek for "a person of practical wisdom." This concept of virtuous people doing virtuous things was carried forward essentially unchanged until the 20th century, when scholars such as Freud began to document how the human psyche grows and changes, particularly from childhood to adulthood. Psychologists now label this process *development*.

Psychologists have empirically documented development on many dimensions, from the acquisition of motor skills in childhood, to the maturation of the human intellect throughout life, and even to some forms of physiological development that express themselves in psychological as well as physical ways. The contemporary understanding suggests that *development* is the result of a complex set of interactions of a dynamic human being living in an equally dynamic external environment. Thus, moral development broadly defined is the notion that how people think about ethical issues will change over time, partly in response to the development of other portions of the individual psyche (e.g., the intellect) and partly in response to the social and cultural environment in which all people find themselves. Moral development expressed through work would be an outgrowth of this larger psychological process.

With this definition and history in mind, it is logical that a psychologist would conduct the first formal investigation of moral development: Jean Piaget, whose book *The Moral Judgment of the Child* provided the academic foundation for the field (Piaget, 1965). Piaget himself described the book as "preliminary" and noted that it followed his work on children's conceptualization of causality. However, both Piaget's method of investigating moral development as well as his findings foreshadowed work in the field for the remainder of the 20th century.

Piaget observed and interviewed Swiss boys as they played marbles—a game with an international following. Piaget's interviews were designed to elicit the boys' understanding of the moral rules, both the practice of those rules and what Piaget described as the "consciousness" of the rules—in other words, whether the rules for marbles were obligatory, sacred, or somehow subject to autonomous human intervention. The use of the word *autonomous* in Piaget's work is significant; philosophers recognize that genuine ethical action begins with an autonomous moral agent. Thus, how such autonomous moral agency developed, although significant for psychology, also had bearing for philosophy.

The boys Piaget observed generally ranged in age from about 5 to 12. Piaget found that as the boys aged their understanding of the rules changed according to a pattern. The very youngest children, age 2, put the marbles in their mouths—a move designed to drive parents crazy but with little moral import other than sensation and exploration. This sort of play, which Piaget characterized as *motor and individual*, led to the formation of more ritualized routines as the children grew older. The play was so highly individual that Piaget believed this stage of development could not truly be characterized as being "cognizant" of the rules. However, contemporary understandings suggest that even adults sometimes do things—and things with moral import—just to "see what it would feel like." When adults engage in such behavior, they may be somewhat conscious of the rules, but they are clearly acting within their own individual understandings. Psychologists would characterize such behavior as reflecting low levels of moral development.

By the time the boys were about 5 or 6, they moved into what Piaget called the *egocentric stage*, in which the child was aware that there was a codified set of rules but continued his highly individualized play. At this stage, even though the children were just beginning to play together, the rules themselves were regarded as sacred and immutable, they emanated from authority figures (usually parents or older boys), and they applied to all— absolutely. Contemporary research suggests that most people, when plunged into a novel situation, will want to learn "the rules" of the game so they can know how to act. Adults can and do respond to novel situations by seeking out guidance in the form of rules.

Between the ages of 7 and 8, however, the boys began to learn to actually play together, what Piaget called the *stage of incipient cooperation*. At this stage, the boys were aware of the rules, although when questioned separately would give quite disparate and often contradictory accounts of the rules themselves. At the early part of this stage, the boys regarded the rules in the same ways as younger children did; in other words, they had a conventional understanding of the rules. However, as they moved through this stage of development, they began to acquire a more sophisticated and internalized conceptualization of the rules. Understanding blossomed in the final stage of development: the *codification of the rules*. In this stage, the boys not only understood the rules and gave the same account of them in separate interviews, they also internalized not just the rules themselves but also the reason for those rules. In other words, the boys had assumed the responsibilities not only for following the rules but for making sure that the spirit of the rules was followed as well.

One particular example provides an illustration of this pattern. Those of you who have played marbles know that the rules dictate that each player shoots his or her marble from outside a circle in which the other marbles have been placed. It is against the rules for the player to begin his or her shot from within the circle. The reason for the circle is an ethical one: It gives everyone an equal shot; it ensures fairness. Yet, when the older boys Piaget studied played marbles with much younger boys, they allowed younger boys to shoot from within the circle. Why? Because the younger boys' hands were weaker. Fairness, the goal of the rule, could be achieved only by allowing the younger boys to shoot from within the circle. Such a decision respected not the letter of the rules, but the reason behind them. The older boys had internalized the reasons for the rules and had exercised both moral autonomy and moral imagination to change the game in such a way as to ensure fairness among unequal parties. Those readers who are familiar with John Rawls' (1971) concept of distributive justice and its foundational principles—maximize liberty and protect the weaker party—will recognize that the boys' solution to inequality in the game of marbles represented some sophisticated reasoning that is also the core of one branch of classical ethical theory.

Piaget's work is important to this volume for four reasons. First, the real-life quality of the game of marbles allowed the boys to demonstrate their understandings in practical ways. This emphasis on real-life practical deci-

sion making suggests that exploring decision making in a professional setting provides a good way to explore moral development. Second, the game
of marbles is inherently visual—something that other studies of moral development have either relegated to the purview of the imagination or minimized by the nature of the moral questions asked. Piaget's work at least
foreshadowed one of the central research questions addressed in this book:
Does visual information make a difference in the kind and quality of ethical
reasoning? Third, Piaget inaugurated the understanding of moral development as proceeding in stages, and that the stages describe a general approach to moral thinking that does not vary depending on the sort of moral
problem presented. Fourth, stage development in Piaget's work is closely
linked to intellectual development. The assertion that moral development
follows distinct stages and is tied to intellectual growth is central to other
studies of moral development, including the one in this book.

Two scholars, both working at Harvard, followed some of Piaget's lead.
Erik Erikson, a psychoanalyst in the Freudian tradition, examined moral development in two ways: through his professional practice and scholarly work
and via his work as a biographer. Erikson built on Piaget's insights about
moral development in childhood by suggesting that developmental stages
continue throughout the life cycle, and that at the core of these developmental stages is a central issue with a moral dimension (Erikson, 1964). Thus,
Erikson theorized that all human beings learn whether they can trust others
when they are infants, and that the acquisition of trust leads to the next developmental stage. Erikson's theory dichotomized each developmental stage.
Thus, infants could learn to trust, but also to mistrust; young adults could
choose intimacy with others or isolation; whereas maturity and old age were
characterized by varying degrees of either ego integrity or despair. There
were eight stages in all, six to be completed by the time a person reached age
25 to 30. In his book *Childhood and Society*, Erikson emphasized the interaction of the individual with the external environment:

> The underlying assumptions are (1) that the human personality in princi-
> ple develops according to steps predetermined in the growing person's
> readiness to be driven toward, to be aware of, and to interact with, a wid-
> ening social radius, and (2) that society, in principle, tends to be so consti-
> tuted as to meet and invite this succession of potentialities for
> interaction and attempts to safeguard and to encourage the proper rate
> and the proper sequence of their enfolding. (Erikson, 1964, p. 270)

Erikson's theory suggested that how each individual works out the conflicts and contradictions at each developmental stage has an impact on how

that individual works out the issues at the next stage. In other words, people can do well or poorly at resolving specific issues, and those individual resolutions will influence how later issues are resolved. This subtlety was not much present in Piaget's work, but it was an important insight. Then, in his Pulitzer Prize-winning biographies (first of Martin Luther and then of Mohandas Gandhi), Erikson demonstrated how the individual resolutions of developmental issues can influence adult actions, and how those adult actions within a culture and society can produce profound moral understanding, action, and—in the cases of both Luther and Gandhi—permanent societal change.

This book also borrows from Erikson. By placing our participants—journalists and journalism students—in a professional context, we assumed that the external environment was significant. In fact, this study asked a lot of questions about the participants' work environment, and, based on the work of Erikson and others, we postulated that work environment would have an effect on their ethical decision making. We also examined whether maturity as reflected by both age and years of professional experience would have an effect on ethical decision making. By focusing on practitioners working in one particular culture (in this case, the United States), we also allowed culture to enter our work. In sum, we assumed that the environment—the individual work environment and the larger cultural environment—mattered.

THE CENTRAL CONTRIBUTIONS OF LAWRENCE KOHLBERG

The second scholar who built on Piaget's work, Lawrence Kohlberg, began researching and writing at Harvard a few years after Erikson. Kohlberg (1976, 1981, 1984) replicated some elements of Piaget's method, although he focused on Harvard undergraduates who, at the time he conducted his research, were all young men. Kohlberg interviewed these Harvard men in depth, querying them about their responses to specific fictional ethical dilemmas that were presented orally. Kohlberg then examined the responses and discovered that, over the course of a Harvard undergraduate education, moral decision making again progressed, again in stages, and those stages in many ways mirrored the developments Piaget had found in younger children.

Kohlberg said his undergraduates moved through three main stages of moral development, each of which could be subdivided into two sequential parts. The first stage was called *preconventional* (a categorization that mirrored Piaget's). Preconventional thinking was subdivided into an initial stage—heteronomous morality, or the display of simple obedience to the rules—and then individualism, or the emergence of self-interest, (e.g., following the rules only when it is in one's self-interest to do so). In this latter half of the preconventional stage, the ethical values of reciprocity and fairness begin to emerge, but only in a self-serving way.

Kohlberg's second stage, which he called *conventional reasoning*, was again subdivided. The first half of the conventional stage was characterized by interpersonal conformity, or doing what other people expect. The second half, however, also included the notion of social systems, or doing what is expected of one to maintain social order. Thinking at this second half of the conventional stage often included thinking about duty, specifically duties to which one had previously agreed. Consideration of duty also has a strong relationship with classical ethical theory.

Finally, Kohlberg's subjects moved to the *postconventional stage*, which was again subdivided. In the first half of the postconventional stage, individual thinking indicated an awareness of the process by which rules were arrived at as well as the content of the rules themselves. The students Kohlberg studied were aware of concepts such as a social contract that demanded citizens to uphold laws even if they were not in an individual's best interest, and the tension between any social contract and individual rights. Thinking at this stage of moral development also included understanding that some "rights"—for example, those of life and liberty—were beyond debate, even if a majority of a society held otherwise. The second half of the postconventional stage, Kohlberg found, was characterized by the individual adoption of universal ethical principles that guided individual choice even if laws were violated. Those at this stage of development had internalized such principles, and they applied them evenhandedly.

Kohlberg's work was extraordinarily influential, particularly among scholars who tried to duplicate both his methods and his results. The Defining Issues Test (DIT) that is one of two central elements of this study was one such effort, and hence it is important to highlight some of Kohlberg's findings because they influenced the development of the DIT. Like both Piaget and Erikson, Kohlberg believed that moral development progressed in stages. The DIT reflects this staged understanding of moral thinking, although it does so with numbers rather than with words. In addition, Kohlberg's work, more than that of Piaget and Erikson, tied moral development to intellectual development and education. This link between education and intellectual development and moral decision making is one of the most robust in all the social science literature about moral development. Even more important, Kohlberg's work emphasized the logical nature of ethical decision making and the logical progression of individual interest to individual rights to individual application of universal principles. This emphasis on logic and the predominant role of the individual is key to understanding Kohlberg's findings. Such an understanding is, by necessity, built into the DIT, particularly into the portion of the DIT that asks respondents to rank reasons for ethical choices. Classical ethical theory, too, emphasizes the role of logic in making ethical choices.

Additionally, Kohlberg's emphasis on duty and rights also reflects two of the major traditions of classical philosophy: utilitarianism, the idea of the greatest good for the greatest number; and deontology, or the notion that ethical actions spring from duty rather than from the character of the individual actor. Immanuel Kant (1785) and W. D. Ross (1930) represent sophisticated thinking about the role of duty in ethical choice; John Stuart Mill (1850, 1861) and Jeremy Bentham are perhaps the best known of the early utilitarian theorists, although Kohlberg also was probably influenced by more contemporary understandings of utilitarianism reflected in John Rawls' (1971) concept of distributive justice. Kohlberg's study, as well as others that followed, found that most people, most of the time, function in the conventional stage of moral development. Rarely did moral thinking emerge at the postconventional level. Because it employs the DIT, this study of journalists' and advertising practitioners' ethical decision making takes Kohlberg's work as an intellectual departure point.

Scholars in various fields have adapted Kohlberg's categories to related concepts. One of the most frequently employed is schema theory, which attempts to explain how people integrate diverse facts into a coherent (for that person) understanding. Schema theory was first employed with infants. Babies were shown two sketches of the human face—the first was what most of us would recognize as a "smiley face," and the second was the same "smiley face" with the eyes and the mouth inverted. Babies under the age of 6 months would smile and coo at both faces; infants older than 6 months would cry when confronted with the upside-down visage. In essence, they had developed a schema for the human face, and reacted accordingly when presented with something that was wrong. Adults employ schemas in similar ways. In fact, psychologists believe that one of the most important roles that schemas play in adult thinking is allowing people to decide which information to integrate into an existing schema and which information to discard. Schemas can be incompletely developed as well as robustly developed. Intuitively, changing an existing schema requires a lot of psychological work.

People have been shown to possess schemas for ethical problems that they use when making decisions about novel ethical problems. Rest, Narvaez,

Bebeau, and Thoma (1999) who developed the DIT, theorized that schemas activated understandings from long-term memory to help people comprehend and process new information that arose from dealing with ethical problems. If a person had acquired a schema for the highest stage of ethical reasoning, some statements from the DIT would activate that schema at that level. Otherwise, lower ethical stage schemas were activated.

Rest, Narvaez, Bebeau, and Thoma (1999) also renamed Kohlberg's stages to more closely fit with the schema concept. What was once Kohlberg's lowest, or preconventional, stage is now called the *personal interest schema* by scholars using the DIT. The definition remains the same; at this stage or schema, the individual is concerned with his or her own welfare. Acts that provide satisfaction to the self and others are "right," but others are considered only when their needs are in line with one's own. Kohlberg's conventional stage—defined by conformity to the expectations of society, where helping others and gaining their approval drives an individual's actions—is now termed the *maintaining norms schema*. The postconventional stage is still called *postconventional*, but with the term *schema* is substituted for *stage*. A comparison of Kohlberg's phases and Rest et al.'s schemas is presented in Table 1.1.

HOW TO INFLUENCE A CRITIC

Kohlberg's work was influential for another reason: Imbedded in it were the seeds of a thoroughgoing criticism of his approach based on both empirical data and the links between real-life choices and ongoing intellectual work in classical philosophy. About 10 years after Kohlberg published the bulk of his findings, another young Harvard graduate student decided to

TABLE 1.1

Kohlberg's Phases and Rest et al.'s Schemas (1999)

	Kohlberg	Rest et al.
Preconventional	Heteronomous moral autonomy	Personal interest
	Individualism	schema
Conventional	Interpersonal conformity	Maintaining norms
	Maintain social order	schema
Postconventional	Awareness of process of rule	Postconventional
	formation	schema
	Universal principles internalized	

put them to a different sort of test. Rather than asking Harvard men about fictional ethical dilemmas, Carol Gilligan (1982) chose to ask women living in the greater Cambridge community about a real-life ethical decision they were making: whether to abort. Her findings, outlined in the book *In a Different Voice*, fundamentally questioned Kohlberg's work on both theoretical and applied levels.

Let's take the theory first. One set of critics suggested that Kohlberg's approach values rational thinking above the actual content of those rational thoughts: "Whether the highest stages of moral reasoning lead to destructive zealotry or real ethicality depends upon the extent to which moral development is matched by development in other sectors," (Keniston, cited in Reid & Yanarella, 1980, p. 121). These scholars have argued that intellect and emotion are equally important components of ethical decision making, and that Kohlberg's approach shortchanges the ethically appropriate influence of emotion.

Other elements of the intellectual foundations for Kohlberg's work were questional as well. However, beginning in the early 1940s (and fueled by the writing of John Jacques Rousseau, the Anabaptists, and others), some philosophers and theologians began to critically reexamine the nature and role of community. In essence, they asserted that individuals could not exist outside of community, and that only within a community could individuals achieve true moral growth. For theologians, such community begins with feeling a oneness with a deity and extends to a oneness with humankind. Political philosophers, who tended to eschew the theological approach, instead suggested that there were certain sorts of issues, those that are generally categorized under the label of *collective goods* (e.g., clean air or water), that could not be justly decided without considering the well-being of the community before the rights of the individual. Feminist philosophers, to some extent working outside both of these traditions as well as within them, suggested that rights without connections to others were hollow. It is not clear to us how much any of these scholars had read and considered the work of Erikson, but Erikson's work certainly foreshadowed this renewed intellectual emphasis on community and culture. Thus, although rights were the philosophical foundation of Kohlberg's work, justice and connection were the intellectual foundations of communitarian and feminist philosophy.

Gilligan had access to much of this work and although she had philosophical reasons to question Kohlberg's approach, she had empirical ones as well. Kohlberg himself, as well as others who had tried to duplicate his research, appeared to find that women in general scored significantly lower on measures of moral development than did men. These researchers also found that very few people functioned at consistently higher levels of moral reasoning. Scholars suggested that a framework that appeared to discriminate between men and women based solely on gender, and on which few people appeared to score in the top ranges, was problematic.

Gilligan asserted that women who were deciding whether to abort spoke literally in a different ethical voice. She found that although Kohlberg's Harvard undergraduates spoke about rights, her women respondents spoke about the necessity for maintaining connections—from the fathers' connections to their unborn children, to the women's bodily connections and psychological ties to the fetuses they carried, to women's connections to their families and friends. Whereas Kohlberg's evaluation criteria tended to overlook such language, Gilligan argued that thinking about connection represented a different, but no less sophisticated, kind of ethical thinking. She and others have called it the *ethics of care*. And although Gilligan concluded that her participants did not progress through stages as first Piaget and then Kohlberg found, the ethical questions the women considered did change as they thought about the problem and their individual relations to it. Gilligan discerned that women first began their moral decision making by considering their responsibilities to care for others before caring for themselves. Then, women began to consider the ethic of rights, including the rights of self to have a say in the ethical choice the women were making. Finally, women moved from a consideration of goodness (care of others) to considerations about universals, particularly truth as a universal principle. (However, not all of the women Gilligan studied considered each of the elements in their ethical thinking.)

Gilligan's findings were just as important as Kohlberg's, and for some of the same reasons. Gilligan's work certainly paralleled developments of the world of academic philosophy and the emergence of communitarianism as a theoretical framework for ethics. However, it is important to note that Aristotle and Mill both thought and wrote about community. Second, Gilligan's research—because it focused on a real as opposed to an imagined dilemma, and because abortion is an issue firmly grounded in intimate connection—allowed those who studied moral development to analyze previous work in a different way.

Gilligan's work, for example, certainly influenced the development and testing of the DIT; on this particular instrument men and women score the same, and in some studies women have scored significantly higher than men. Gilligan's work also questioned the whole notion of staged moral development. Gilligan did not describe her research subjects as moving through stages; rather, they reached different insights at different times in their thinking. This insight, of asking different questions at different times in the thinking process, has influenced the analysis of the data presented in this book. The larger issue—Do people progress through stages of moral growth?—continues to be a vibrant intellectual question. One might hope that age would bring wisdom; whether one should expect it in a social scientific sense remains open to debate.

Finally, Gilligan gave scholars another way to look at the reasons behind the rules. In most of her writing since the original book, Gilligan has suggested that true moral adulthood requires reasoning both according to the ethics of rights and responsibilities and thinking about care—both with the intellect and the heart. The moral adult, Gilligan has asserted, needs to be able to reason both ways, and to discern when specific frameworks are appropriate. Studies following Gilligan's lead have suggested that both men and women exercise the ethics of care as well as the ethics of rights and responsibilities. Aristotle would not have disagreed with this characterization of a "person of practical wisdom." In many studies, including those using the DIT, both women and men can and do reach the stages of moral development at which universal principles (of care and rights) become internalized. As of this writing, no scholar that we are aware of has developed a written instrument to "test" Gilligan's conceptualization of moral thinking. Developing and testing such an instrument would be a contribution to academic work in many fields. However, even though such an instrument does not currently exist, how Gilligan listened to and interpreted the "voices" of her participants has influenced the analysis of the voices of journalists who are the focus of this work.

On the most basic level, Gilligan's contributions have made it important to ask whether women score differently than men on any portion of the current project, and whether there are other descriptive characteristics of our samples—age, education, length of time in the profession—that make a difference in how people respond. At the analytic level, Gilligan's work has allowed us to ask questions such as: How should one interpret a reason centered in the First Amendment that could reflect reliance on rules (a lower level of moral development) or an ethic of care about the role of free speech in a democracy (a universal principle that incorporates both care and rights). Gilligan's empirical work understood in conjunction with developments in philosophy, also prompts questions about justice as a foundational value for journalists. The justice issues that emerge from communitarian and feminist philosophy are particularly meaningful when race and ethnicity become the focus of ethical decision making. This, too, influenced the analysis in this book.

Although all these studies—from Piaget to Kohlberg through Gilligan—have examined moral development from various theoretical perspectives, their methodological similarities are also worth noting. All the studies (with the exception of the DIT) worked with small groups of either children or adults. Intensive, in-depth, longitudinal interviewing was the predominant research method. None of these scholars made any attempt to generalize to all children or all adults; indeed, the issue of generalizability across gender remains one impetus for Gilligan's work and scholarly acceptance of it. Samples have been small by traditional social science standards; indeed, some studies appear more psychoanalytic than psychological in approach. However, many of the findings in this work appear both internally and externally consistent. Never in the history of research in moral development has there been an attempt to generalize to the adult population at large in the same fashion as, for example, electoral polls and surveys. Although in the next chapter we discuss methodology in detail, it is important for readers of this book to understand that the methodological approach taken here follows the general approach of more than 60 years of study on this issue. Whereas this book emphasizes accepted standards of intellectual rigor in what is generally a social science orientation, we have also held to the approach and methods of scholars whose work has influenced our own.

The foregoing has briefly summarized the linchpins of research in moral development. In addition, it has connected elements of these seminal works to this particular study of journalists. However, there are other contributing strands in our fabric of knowledge about human moral growth; most are not as well integrated into the generally accepted academic literature, but each is important to our efforts and thinking. A review of that work follows.

CONTEMPORARY INSIGHTS: IMPORTANT ISSUES FOR REFLECTION

We begin this section with something that's not quite so contemporary—unless you are an academic philosopher. In 1968, William Perry published his book, *Intellectual Growth and Development in the College Years*, which added support to the notion that moral development moves in tandem with intellectual growth. Perry also studied Harvard men throughout their undergraduate educations, and found that intellectually these men moved from a stance of reliance on an authority figure for "the right" answer and for knowledge, through stages that progressed to a final stage at which the young men were able to make an intellectual commitment to a life work. Although Perry's work examined intellectual development, his discussion of the role of authority and intellectual autonomy in student development and the concluding developmental stage of "commitment lived" clearly parallels findings in the literature of moral development. Perry set out to ask slightly different questions than Kohlberg did; the answers he found were remarkably consistent with Kohlberg's work.

More than 20 years after Perry wrote, four of Carol Gilligan's graduate students studied intellectual development among adult women—none of whom appeared to be facing a specific ethical crisis. Their book, *Women's Ways of Knowing* (Belenky et al., 1986), just like Perry's, had implications for work in moral development—some of them quite contradictory to earlier findings in the field. Those contradictions begin with the method itself. Like Gilligan, the authors focused on women, but unlike their mentor, they deliberately chose women who varied in age from 20 to 60, came from lower socioeconomic as well as middle-class backgrounds, and included African American women among their 24-person research cohort. In this approach, they appeared to put to empirical test Erikson's assertions that environment and life experience can make a difference; indeed, this is what they found. Women of color who were poor demonstrated much less sophisticated intellectual development, although there were some exceptions. Education made an enormous difference in how the women developed intellectually. As well, there were some women who provided the researchers with little evidence of intellectual growth through time. Contrary to the notion of predictable stages through which the women progressed as they aged, the authors of *Women's Ways of Knowing* found that some women got "stuck" in particular intellectual stages from which they never emerged. Getting "stuck" wasn't purely intellectual; women who suffered physical abuse either at the hands of spouses or through rape had a much more difficult time making progress, although, again, there were exceptions.

Although the focus of the study was intellectual development, the researchers themselves found that the women dealt with ethical issues among many others in their lives. Their findings partially buttressed Kohlberg's assertion that most people function in the mid-range of moral development, although the study could also be read as a partial repudiation of that finding. Clearly, there was a dynamic involved in moral development among adults that earlier studies had either discounted in the search for theoretical parsimony or had never found because college-age men were the primary research cohorts.

The implications of this work for the study you are about to read are straightforward; it was important for us to ask about life experience in general and life experience defined by certain characteristics (e.g., ethnicity). It was equally important for us to assume that development was not automatic—nor that journalists could be "stuck" in predictable reasoning patterns for significant reasons. Finally, the work in *Women's Ways of Knowing* also raised the question of the emotional and experiential component of moral growth, something that previous work, with the exception of Erikson and Gilligan, had tended to minimize.

The emotional component of moral development has been the focus of significant work as well. This focus represents a departure from some understandings of classical ethical theory, which tends to emphasize logic. Feminist ethical theory, as well as the traditional Judeo / Christian approach to ethics, does incorporate an element of emotion—love—but how emotion aids or retards moral development has been the subject of some study and little consensus. Perhaps the best-researched area of the field has been empathy and how it develops and then contributes to prosocial behavior. Some of this work has been done with infants and young children and employs visual stimuli; other studies working with older children have used verbal dilemmas. Studies have found that children as well as adults respond to situations with what is called *empathic distress*—in other words, they form an emotional response to the representation of the victim's life condition and the victim's likely responses to that condition. Studies indicate that empathic distress can be generalized to entire classes of people; for example, the poor or victims of war. Scholars suggest that empathy is congruent with an ethic of care and that it has implications for distributive justice: "While empathy may not make a structural contribution to justice, it may provide the motive to rectify violations of justice of others" (Hoffman, 2000, p. 228).

Thus, the concept of empathy has a clear connection with classical ethical theory, particularly the work of John Rawls and much feminist theory as well as communitarianism. Scholarly studies of empathy have associated the concept with motivation to behave in an ethical, or sometimes a superogatory, manner. However, this same body of literature does not clearly connect the development of empathy to any particular stage of moral development, although by inference the development of empathy would certainly be present at higher stages of moral development. For purposes of this study, the fact that some scholars have used visual information to provoke an emotional response provided another important theoretical reason to test the effect of visual information on ethical thinking. Searching for signs of empathy, particularly in the open-ended part of the study, also was an important analytic approach.

The work on empathy also raises the issue of motivation. The great bulk of work on moral development, extending from Piaget and to Gilligan, suggests that internalization of ethical principles is an important marker of moral development. Indeed, in the work of Piaget and Kohlberg, internalization defines movement from a lower to a higher developmental stage. Many people, scholars among them, have noted that people will often say one thing and do another, and moral development theory cannot account for this human paradox. Scholars have suggested that a partial reason for this dichotomy may be the fact that human beings appear to internalize different aspects of their lives at different rates. Then, people must conduct that psychological work of integrating this now-internal understanding into their behavior—a difficult task for anyone, let alone someone who is working on deadline. Although we could not "test" whether people would say one thing and then do another in the newsroom, we could evaluate whether they appeared to be internally or externally motivated to act ethically. Based on the scholarship in the field, we theorized that internal motivation might be one additional indicator of higher rather than lower levels of moral development, and that internal motivation might express itself in the reasons that journalists gave for their ethical choices.

Finally, during the course of conducting this study, another study of journalists and ethics—a book titled *Good Work*—entered the literature of the field (Gardner, Csikszentmihalyi, & Damon, 2001). This investigation, conducted by three psychologists, used a research method called a *Q sort* to ask a panel of 100 journalists, all of whom were characterized as leaders in the field, how they would define "good work." The answers and tensions that emerged from these conversations with journalists certainly included ethical reflection. More specifically, these conversations spoke both to an ethic of journalistic rights and responsibilities and an ethic of care—or stewardship—for a profession that many of the journalists believed is under powerful economic pressure. The findings in *Good Work* also support some of the findings in this volume.

THE PRESENT EFFORT: THE RESEARCH QUESTIONS

Based on the previous literature that combined psychology, academic philosophy, and applied professional ethics, the study you are about to read asked the following questions:

- As professionals, how would journalists and advertising practitioners score on the DIT, and how would their scores compare with those of members of other professions who have taken this test in the last 30 years?
- Were there any predictable patterns in the journalists' and advertising practitioners' scores? For example, did women score differently than men, did those who had worked as journalists for a long time score differently than those who were novices, did print journalists differ from broadcasters, and so on?
- If visual information were an added component of the ethical dilemmas presented to journalists, did it appear to have any effect?
- When journalists wrote about the decisions they made, what sort of moral development became apparent? Was there evidence of schematic thinking? Was there evidence of an ethic of rights or an ethic of care?
- Does culture—either of the newsroom or of the advertising agency—appear to play a role in ethical decision making?
- Do those who are motivated internally make different decisions or give different reasons for their ethical choices than do those who are motivated externally?

The next chapter explains the method in detail.

CHAPTER 2

Methods: Multiple Approaches to Asking Questions

This book was based on several studies of journalists' ethical reasoning using two main types of research—two large-scale surveys and several, smaller experiments. The foundation of this research was a survey of 249 professional journalists who completed the Defining Issues Test (DIT) plus an accompanying questionnaire. A second DIT survey focused on advertising practitioners. A third survey, examining the particular ethical issue of deception, was administered to members of the professional organization Investigative Reporters and Editors (IRE). Although all surveys were designed to generate quantitative data, each also included a segment of what scholars refer to as *qualitative data*—journalists were allowed to explain their thinking using their own words and concepts. Based on the survey results, experiments were then devised to examine in a more controlled way whether visual images would influence ethical reasoning. It is important to note at the outset that although the general subject matter—ethical reasoning—was the center of the research, the multiple methods employed focused on distinct aspects of the larger research question. The following explanation not only outlines the specific studies but also provides the reasoning behind research decisions.

THE SURVEY: BORROWING AND EXPANDING ON THE PSYCHOLOGICAL TRADITION

Quantitative researchers like to say they can measure anything—a person's intelligence, creativity, even cognitive development. To explore journalists' moral development, we used a 30-year-old test that measures the quality of reasoning individuals use when faced with ethical dilemmas. Its full name is the arcane-sounding "Defining Issues Test," but researchers in the field collapse the letters into an acronym—the DIT. The DIT was devised by psychologists in the 1970s and has been administered to more than 20,000 people in different professions, including doctors, dentists, nurses, veterinarians, and even prison inmates. It is the most frequently used quantitative instrument measuring moral development, and literally hundreds of scholarly studies, as well as several books, have been published using the DIT as an intellectual backbone.

Those who take the DIT know the test is about ethics. However, one of the things that makes it a valuable research tool is that test takers cannot discern which answers are "better" than others. When taking the DIT, participants read six stories about ethical dilemmas, among them Lawrence Kohlberg's classic quandary about whether a poor man, Heinz, is ethically justified in stealing a drug that will save his mortally ill wife's life, but which a pharmacist has declined to "give" him for free and which he cannot afford to buy. After choosing whether to recommend Heinz steal the drug, participants then read 12 different statements and rate how important each one was in making their decision. For instance, one person might think it very important to consider whether stealing, in this case, would bring about more total good for society, thus making the druggist's rights of lesser importance. Others taking the test might evaluate these competing claims differently. After reading and rating 12 such statements, participants then narrow their most important choices and rank the top 4 in order of importance.

The 12 statements reflect Kohlberg's three stages of ethical reasoning, ranging from the highest or "principled" ethical reasoning, through the most common or "conventional" ethical reasoning, to the lowest or "preconventional" ethical reasoning (reviewed in chap. 1). The researchers can then evaluate respondents' answers and calculate what percentage of the time a particular respondent uses the highest level of principled ethical reasoning. The result of that calculation is called a P score. Most adults use this type of reasoning (principled as opposed to conventional or preconventional) about 40% of the time. Since the DIT was developed, aggregate P scores have been compiled for many professions and for the general population.

There are obvious questions about the DIT, or any other paper-and-pencil test that measures complex mental functioning. (Readers interested in a critical approach to this issue are encouraged to read Stephen J. Gould's *The Mismeasure of Man* which discusses the uses and misuses of the IQ test for the past 100 years.) One of the most fundamental is whether the test is measuring what it says it is—in this case, moral development—and not something else like education or reading ability. The DIT has been tested for validity—in other words, that it measurers what it says it measures—in more than 400 published studies (Rest et al., 1999). It also has some built-in checks and balances. For example, there's an internal check to make sure the statements a respondent says are of most importance in his or her decision also show up in the part of the test where the same respondent ranks the four most important choices. People who include too many "little importance" statements in their top-four list have their questionnaires thrown out. Scholars also have found that people who wanted to appear "more ethical" selected statements that sounded important. Hence, among the 12 statements included in the DIT are some that sound impressive but are really nonsense (e.g., "Whether the essence of living is more encompassing than the termination of dying"). If a respondent chooses too many like that, his or her questionnaire is also thrown out. In the 30 years or so that the DIT has been administered, about 8% of the people tested picked too many meaningless statements and their responses have been disregarded. The effect of these checks is that respondents are able to "fake" a lower level of moral development, but not a higher one without choosing too many of those meaningless items (Davison & Robbins, 1978; Rest, 1979).

Scholars aware of the research on both social desirability bias and common sense suggest why these checks are important. Most people would not want to be considered "less" ethical; hence, deliberately low scores are less likely to occur. On the other hand, no matter how much a respondent wants to be considered "more" ethical, "faking high" is difficult because of the construction of the test. The DIT is also highly reliable, with Cronbach's alpha in the high .70s and low .80s. Those who take it once are likely to get a similar score if they take it again.

The DIT is specifically applicable to journalism in two ways. First, one of the original six dilemmas incorporated into the DIT involves journalism. Second, up to two of the DIT dilemmas can be replaced with stories that researchers create. This survey took advantage of that opportunity by including two new dilemmas about journalism, one broadcast related and one print related. Advertising scenarios also were created and incorporated into the survey given to advertising practitioners. The advertising-specific scenarios focused on stereotyping and diversity in advertising content and the decision of whether to help market a controversial product.

The scenarios created for journalists had a second research purpose: testing the effect of imagined and actual visual information on ethical reasoning. The first of the new journalism additions involved the use of hidden cameras; the second whether to run a controversial photograph after someone associated with the story asked that it not be used (see Fig. 2.1). This dilemma included the actual photograph for both craft and intellectual reasons. Research indicates that visual images are processed on the right side of the brain whereas verbal work is done on the left side. Would having a photograph—which would be processed on the right side of the brain—affect ethical thinking? Would imagining visual images—those collected from the hidden camera—have any impact? From the craft standpoint, it was important to make the dilemma as real as possible; including an actual news photograph accomplished that. Previously, the only DIT dilemmas customized for journalists that dealt with visual issues did not include actual photographs (Westbrook, 1995).

After they worked through the six ethical dilemmas, the respondents answered a three-page questionnaire. This part of the research focused on participants' motivations and the kinds of things previous studies suggested would influence ethical reasoning—for example, how much choice or autonomy the participants had at work, religious beliefs and political ideology, journalists' involvement with civic journalism and investigative reporting, how many professional organizations participants belonged to or how many seminars they attended, and the usual demographics of size of organization, years as a journalist or advertising practitioner, job title, age, gender, and race. This information allowed an examination of the internal and external factors related to levels of ethical thinking. It also permitted

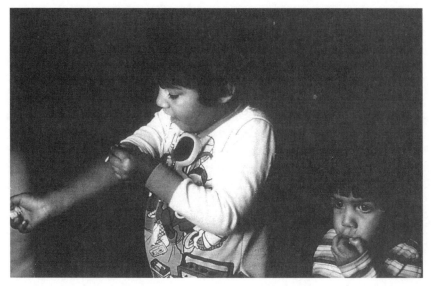

FIG. 2.1

some basic comparisons, such as men and women, broadcasters and print journalists, civic journalists and investigative reporters, journalists and advertising practitioners.

DECIDING WHOM TO STUDY

It is risky to write in general terms about the ethical reasoning of U.S. journalists because they are so diverse (for demographics, see Weaver, Beam, Brownlee, Voakes, & Wilhoit, in press). Characterizing advertising and public relations practitioners runs into a similar set of difficulties. As research scholars note, if you don't have some idea about the boundaries of the population you are studying, it becomes difficult to know whether results describe and analyze whom and what they are attempting to represent. It is even riskier to try to talk generally when the data have been collected in some other way than the social science gold standard: random sampling. The first and most extensive survey on which this book is based was not random in the sense that every single journalist working in the United States would have an equal chance of being included. Random surveys give researchers some measure of confidence that the results accurately represent the population from which they were drawn, and allow the researchers to calculate just how far off their data might be. In other words, randomness can be one check against "bad data." Statistically, results are generalized—applied to those who did not participate in the survey—with a certain level of confidence. The efficiency and reliability of random sampling has been proven again and again.

However, random sampling is not always an appropriate research choice. The information on which a major portion of this book is based was collected using a nationwide, *representative* sample of 249 professional journalists. Representative sampling is one of the nonprobability sampling techniques commonly used in journalism research. We chose a representative sample because of the kind of topic being researched—ethical thinking; because the kind of research instrument used—the DIT; and because although random sampling is good for gauging things like political opinion or media use, it is much less effective if the question involved focuses on the thinking process.

Instead, the 249 journalists in the large survey were chosen with a technique called multistage cluster sampling. This approach basically determines what groups or clusters of characteristics are important to the population and then matches participants on those characteristics. To determine the important clusters or subsets of the population of U.S. journalists, we used the most recent national, random samples of working journalists as a guide (Weaver & Wilhoit, 1996; Weaver et al., in press). We began with geographic region and developed lists of news organizations in the West, South, North, and Midwest using the 2001 and 2002 *Editor & Publisher* and *Broadcasting & Cable* yearbooks. Next, we categorized the news outlets by size using the newspaper circulation categories of large (more than 100,000), medium (25,000 to 100,000), and small (less than 25,000). Broadcast market sizes are roughly comparable—bigger TV stations and larger circulation newspapers are found in the same cities—and using circulation sizes of newspapers afforded more precision. Letters were written to top managers of news organizations in each category from each geographic region explaining the study; up to three follow-up calls were made asking for permission to conduct on-site visits to administer the DIT.

Next, we identified the categories shown to be important in moral development or for other things—age and education are the most important predictors of moral development, and race, gender, and political party are important in almost everything else. Because it was impossible to obtain lists of all working journalists, we selected individuals in the same proportion of the population on these categories. Babbie (1990) said this is "likely to be more representative on a number of variables than would be the case for a simple random sample" (p. 87), and others have noted that this is "a promising way to make the connection between the universe" (Kane, 2002). To accomplish this, we analyzed the demographic data after each round of data collection; typically, one to three newsrooms per site were visited with 5 to 20 journalists from each newsroom participating. This allowed us to modify the selection of news organizations for the next wave of data collection in order to conform to the proportions of individuals in the population. For example, if we found we had more journalists age 20 to 24, we would next visit larger news outlets where older journalists were typically found.

We were interested in maintaining proportions at the *individual* level, not the *organizational* level, so this modification resulted in a sample that was potentially more in proportion to the population of individual U.S. journalists than a simple random sample of news organizations.

However, the journalists who participated in this research do reflect the broad demographic characteristics of the largest random sample of journalists conducted in the past decade (Weaver & Wilhoit, 1996). For example, according to Weaver et al. (in press), 70% of journalists work in print media, 29% in broadcast, and 1% at news services; the journalists in this study mirror those percentages. Furthermore, Weaver et al. (in press) found that 38% of U.S. journalists work in the South, 25% in the Midwest, 20% in the Northeast, and 17% in the West. The journalists in this study come from news organizations in those regions in roughly the same percentages. The news organizations that participated also reflect the actual distribution of newspapers and television stations by size (circulation and market) as determined by the American Society of Newspaper Editors.

This study also closely matched journalists on individual characteristics that are reviewed in detail in the next chapter. Although these comparisons are important in terms of making certain that the journalists involved in this study represent working journalists as a whole, it's crucial to note that, with the exception of age and education, the literature on moral development fails to link individual demographic differences or geographic location with differences in ethical thinking.

Because of the purposive sampling of journalists at the individual level, this is not a probability sample; however, that should not discount the results for several reasons. Recall that our intention is not generalization but comparison, for which Babbie (1990) says a nonprobability multistage sample design is sufficient. Our method of data collection is appropriate for comparison with studies of other professions because almost none of the more than 400 DIT studies in the past 30 years are random samples, and almost all were administered in person by researchers. Never in the history of moral development research has there been an attempt to generalize to the population in the same way as electoral polls and surveys.

It has been recognized that when probability sampling is not feasible, nonprobability sampling is acceptable (Babbie, 1990). Probability and generalizability theorists have debated the use of representative sampling instead of random sampling and concluded that if it can be plausibly claimed that the sample is representative of a specified universe, and that selective forces that might introduce bias have been minimized (Cronbach, Gleser, Nanda, & Rajaratnam, 1972; Kane, 2002), then "such a sample can be accepted as being equivalent to a truly random sample" (Langley, 1970, p. 49). Stratification, such as we have done, "can make a major contribution to our confidence that the sample" is representative (Kane, 2002, p. 175). Cook and Campbell go farther and suggest that "deliberate sampling for heterogeneity" in which "a wide range of instances from within each class represented in the design" enhances external validity (Cook & Campbell, 1979, p. 75).

Finally, Riffe, Lacy, and Fico (1998) noted that there are three conditions that justify the use of nonprobability sampling. First, "the material being studied must be difficult to obtain" (Riffe et al., 1998, p. 85). This is certainly true of an "ethics test." Ethics is quite possibly the hardest topic to get journalists—or anyone, for that matter—to talk about in an intimate, personal way. The difficulty of obtaining such information explains why almost all empirical research on actual ethical decision making employs retrospective individual case studies, participant observation within newsrooms, or very small samples of journalists. Only one researcher before us has ever attempted to use the DIT on journalists (Westbrook, 1995), and those results remain in an unpublished doctoral dissertation. The DIT questions are much more complex than are demographic questions or self-report responses to questions about influences on ethical behavior (Weaver & Wilhoit, 1996).

The second condition that justifies a nonprobability sample occurs when "resources limit the ability to generate a random sample of the population" (Riffe et al., 1998, p. 85). Initially, we attempted to mail our research instrument to news organizations at which we had personal contacts. The results were dismal; out of 100 surveys mailed, about 12 were returned. The conundrum here is that for a random sample to be valid, it must achieve a response rate of at least 60%; anything less is no better than a convenience sample. It became clear that mailed surveys were not going to generate that sort of response rate. In order to get journalists to complete the survey, the DIT needed to be administered in person, and a cursory examination of all DIT studies show that indeed this instrument is almost always administered by the researchers in person. This study adopted that approach. The researchers arrived at news organizations bearing lunch, and the journalists who participated in the study completed the DIT during their lunch hour. This approach was less disruptive of often busy and fragmented workdays, and it allowed for some advance planning. (Few journalists saw the irony in an ethics test that required a bribe.) Had a statistically random sample been the methodological goal, in-person survey administration would have required visits to about 150 locations across the country, a physical and financial impossibility. In fact, most random samples are collected either by phone or mail; neither of these were reasonable possibilities for this version of the DIT (which included the photograph) and the attached questionnaire. Advertising practitioners took the DIT on the Web, an advantage for data collection that produced a confounding variable of another sort—whether the way the survey was administered would have an effect on the results.

The third condition justifying nonprobability sampling is "when a researcher is exploring some under researched but important area" (Riffe et al., 1998, p. 85). This research meets this criteria because journalists are one of a very few professional groups for which baseline ethical reasoning data have yet to be collected. Almost every type of profession that must grapple with significant ethical issues has been studied in this context, but not journalism. With these data, we will be able to compare the reasoning of journalists with the reasoning of other professionals. This study is unique; no one has ever studied the ethical reasoning of journalists or advertising practitioners in this manner.

For all these reasons—some of them quite practical but all of them informed by the theory surrounding research methods in general and the DIT in particular—a representative sample was the optimal research approach. Findings from a representative sample cannot be conclusively generalized to the entire population of U.S. journalists; however, a carefully selected representative sample, and results that mirror or advance the findings of other scholars, are certainly strongly suggestive of more generalized understandings. It was not the intention of this study to generalize to the population in the sense that random sample surveys do, but to replicate others' results. Replication is an effective way to control for selective forces in nonrandom samples; if several studies involving different samples yield the same pattern of results, then either the same selection biases are operating across the replications, or they are not having a major effect on the results (Kane, 2002). Cook and Campbell say the "external validity is enhanced more by a number of smaller studies with haphazard samples than by a single study with initially representative samples" (1979, p. 73). This is the third study of journalists, and the three results are consistent. As is traditional with DIT studies, generalizable statements become possible after many smaller studies of different participants from the same profession have been conducted over time. As the third such study of journalists, this represents one more step in a cumulative process of knowledge acquisition about journalists' ethical development. This book is intended to be the genesis of a course of study that, we hope, will engage others and continue for many years to provide a truly in-depth and complete picture of how media professionals reason about ethics.

Finally, a word about the size of this representative sample. In studies that employ the DIT, samples of 100 or fewer are the norm; this representative sample more than doubles that number. Furthermore, it is a statistical idiosyncrasy that when a sample exceeds 200, results tend to become redundant rather than provide genuinely new information. Given the law of large numbers, a large sample simply for the sake of a large sample will certainly ensure statistical significance, but it will probably not add to the meaning and depth of the results.

PUTTING ON THE PRESSURE:
THE NEED FOR EXPERIMENTS

The pilot study of the survey provided information of one sort—descriptive data about ethical reasoning with tantalizing findings; visual information appeared to make some difference in ethical thinking. When philosophers encounter a provocative line of reasoning with multiple alternative paths of analysis, they "put a little pressure" on the thinking to see if a clearer line of thought emerges. We did the same thing to investigate the effect of visual information.

We chose to conduct experiments for several reasons. Unlike surveys, interviews, or focus groups, experiments are the only way to establish causality. It was important to test whether visual information caused a change in ethical reasoning and to attempt to describe that change. With experiments, we could control other possible causes, such as the race and ages of the people in the photos and the social problem that the news story explored. The results of these experiments are outlined in chapters 5 and 6 of this volume.

Journalism majors at three universities—two in the Midwest and a third in the South—participated; half of them saw photographs with the ethical dilemmas and half did not. The level of ethical reasoning between the two groups was then compared. A technique called "random assignment" determined which participants received dilemmas with photographs and which did not. To do this, the order of the test with photos and the test without photos was varied completely at random, so all participants had an equal chance of receiving visual information. Although not the same thing, random assignment in experiments performs a similar function as does random sampling in survey research. Random assignment helps ensure that characteristics important to the research are normally distributed within each experimental group, much as they are in the general population. Use of random assignment makes the need for random sampling a moot point in experimental research.

The use of college students as subjects for experiments has been widely accepted in mass media research—indeed, in psychological and social science research in general. One estimate is that 75% of all mass media experiments involve student subjects. Obviously, a sample of students is not representative of the population, nor does it need to be. The distinction revolves around research with the goal of generalizability (e.g., surveys) and research with the purpose of establishing causality (e.g., experiments). If experimental effects are indeed found in the samples of college students, then it may be assumed that these same effects may be found in the population of professional journalists and that group may then be included in the research. At this stage, however, we make no claims to being representative of professional journalists at large in the reports on the findings of the experiments.[1]

Furthermore, although the sample was made up of college students, it was purposely limited to journalism students in an effort to approximate the thought processes of journalists. It should also be considered that students at the University of Missouri School of Journalism, who made up two thirds of the experimental cohort, are not typical of journalism students at most schools—many have significant professional experience before entering school. Two years of professional experience is generally a requirement for admission to the graduate program; even undergraduates tend to have worked at local and school media to gain an edge for admission. Furthermore, once they are admitted to the program, students are required to work in the newsrooms of the newspaper, magazine, or television station that are run by the school but serve the entire community. Although there no doubt are differences between professional journalists and aspiring journalists, it is not unreasonable to suppose that professional journalists, too, would exhibit similar processing of ethical issues, especially young journalists, who make up the bulk of newsworkers in many media today.

In the first experiment, two of the four dilemmas asked people to decide whether to publish a photograph after someone associated with the subject of the photograph had requested it not be run. This scenario was patterned after an actual case (Borden, 1996) in which a newspaper was asked by a third party, on behalf of the family, not to run a photograph. In that actual case, journalists made the decision without ever seeing the photograph. In the experiment, half the participants made the decision exactly the same way those journalists did—without the photograph. The other half of the participants were able to refer to the photograph. It should be noted that, in many newsrooms, ethical decisions regarding visual content are made both ways. The other scenarios created for the experiments also closely paralleled actual news stories, including photographs that did, in fact, illustrate actual news stories, although not the same ones as in this study's dilemmas.

In the other two dilemmas, the decision to be made was whether a journalist should run a story when none of the sources would go "on the record." It turned out that the type of decision a person had to make— whether to use anonymous sources or a photograph that might offend—

---

[1]For further justification of using college students in experimental research, see also Basil (1996) and Courtright (1996). This is a rather well-worn subject; the consensus of those who correctly conduct and understand the purpose of experimental research and how it differs from survey research is to accept the use of students as necessary and not particularly compromising of the results.

did not have a statistically significant influence on moral thinking. Thus, in the next set of experiments, all the dilemmas were streamlined to ask whether to run the photograph. All the dilemmas presented in these experiments were designed to have no single clear ethical answer. In all cases, powerful arguments could be made for the ethicality of running the photograph or not, using the story without naming sources or not. The focus in these exercises was placed on the quality of the reasoning used in the decision-making process, not on the decision itself.

The photographs the participants saw had won prestigious national awards (Pictures of the Year), so quality was not an issue. If the photographs had been of average or poor quality, either aesthetically or technically, then participants might have focused their reasoning on craft values rather than ethical issues. The photographs were compelling but not graphic, thereby mitigating other potential craft responses, such as "This photograph will make readers uncomfortable and so should not be published." All photographs were black and white to control for the effects of color, which can add drama to sensitive images (Lester, 1991). Finally, these photographs were chosen because they added something to the story that could not be conveyed by written text alone—the power of emotion and depth of understanding that only a visual image can provide.

Unlike the original DIT survey, which had one newspaper dilemma and one broadcast dilemma, all dilemmas in these experiments were set in a newspaper of unspecified size. This was done to control for possible perceived ethical differences between print and broadcast media, and between local and national media outlets. It is widely agreed that ethical choices that are acceptable at large metropolitan media organizations would be protested vehemently by audiences and journalists alike at smaller, local media outlets (Husselbee & Adams, 1996).

In summary, the results of the DIT survey taken by journalists, as well as the literature of the field, suggested that visual information might influence ethical thinking. We devised experiments to test this theory and to discover whether visual information elevated or diminished the level of ethical thought.

A WORD ABOUT RACE

In the first two experiments, the potential effect of race was controlled by presenting two pictures of African Americans and two of Caucasians. We reasoned that because all participants who saw photographs saw people of all races, participants would basically act as their own controls—that is, any individual differences due to seeing people of a certain race would be canceled out by also seeing people of another race. We also gave the people in the stories names that were ethnically ambiguous, so that participants who didn't see photographs would not infer race.

Despite these efforts, what we found troubled us; this is explained in more detail in chapter 5. But, again, it was impossible to determine if race was causing the results, and, just as we had done with the visual information, we "put some pressure" on these findings as well by devising a third set of experiments. That study is discussed in detail in chapter 6.

In conclusion, there are several important advantages to experiments. Experiments are the only way to identify the cause of some effect. The use of random assignment to condition and a control group (in this case, people who didn't see photos) helps rule out alternative explanations. Such analysis cannot be accomplished using other research methods, even if the participants are randomly sampled.

The ability to replicate experiments is another advantage. As with any research, no one study will ever provide conclusive answers, even those that use random sampling. Rather, it is a preponderance of evidence, collected over time using different populations, under different conditions, in different settings, by different researchers, that provides greater confidence in making statements about phenomena, whether they be cause-and-effect relationships or generalizations about a population. By asking questions about ethical thinking in different ways, of different but professionally related groups of people, some overall understanding can emerge. That is the goal of the remainder of this volume.

CHAPTER 3

Context and Results: The Defining Issues Test

THEORETICALLY INFORMED APPLICATION

Some background in the study of moral development is essential to understanding the DIT and what it examines. As indicated previously, the DIT is the most widely used paper-and-pencil test of moral development. Because it has been administered so many times to so many different types of people, a brief review of general findings from those studies will provide some perspective to understanding how journalists fared.

First, let's take a look at how demographics correlate with DIT results. According to Rest (1986, 1993), age and education are the primary determinants of moral development. Longitudinal studies have found significant changes in DIT scores from high school into adulthood (Rest, 1983; White, Bushnell, & Regnemer, 1978). Data suggest that moral development plateaus when formal education stops (Rest 1979b).

Gender as a determinant of moral development has been studied extensively, but with arguable results. As noted in chapter 1, one of the enduring criticisms of Kohlberg's work is an inherent bias toward men. Since Gilligan's (1982) initial studies, gender has been a focus of much scholarship. However, when it comes to the DIT, a review shows that more than 90% of all DIT studies find no gender differences (Rest, 1979a). When differences do exist, better explanations are offered by differences in educational opportunities (Rest, 1983). Other studies find a difference, but with women consistently scoring significantly higher than men (see for a meta-analysis, Thoma, 1986). Thus, it is important for this study to examine the effects of age, education, and gender on the results.

At least as contentious as gender is the impact of religion on moral development. Intuitively, most people probably assume that people who are more religious, or people who say that religion is very important in their thinking, would do well on a test that asks them to think about "good" behavior, something for which all religions call. Indeed, religion is positively correlated with moral development. However, that correlation extends only so far. More fundamental or conservative religious beliefs have been correlated with lower levels of moral development in numerous studies (Lawrence, 1978; Parker, 1990; Rest 1979, 1983, 1986). Many scholars theorize that a higher ethical orientation requires critical and evaluative reasoning. Such a mindset may clash with fundamentalist religious beliefs (Parker, 1990). Similarly, Glock and Stark (1996) found that orthodox Christian beliefs were highly correlated with social intolerance, and Ellis' (1986) work led to the conclusion that religiosity leads to an extreme disregard for the rights of others. Obviously, examining what journalists say about their religious beliefs is an important component in understanding why participants scored the way they did.

Far less contentious is the effect of membership in professional organizations. Moral development is correlated with peer interaction such as participation in clubs and special activity groups, and service in leadership roles (Harris, Mussen, & Rutherford, 1976; Keasey, 1971; Kohlberg, 1958). Much of this work has been done with children rather than adults, however, so generalizing this finding to adults is a bit of a reach. Participants in this research were asked to indicate how many professional organizations they belonged to and how many professional conferences they had attended in the past year. In the business fields, research has shown that managers tend to score lower than do nonmanagers and entrepreneurs (Allen & Ng, 2001; Teal & Carroll, 1999).

Besides studies of the kinds of things that influence moral development in other professions, the field of journalism has examined a variety of influences on journalists' ethical reasoning. For example, external influences such as laws and organizational policies have consistently been correlated to ethical decision making by journalists (Black, Barney, & Van Tubergen, 1979; Singletary, Caudill, Caudill, & White, 1990; Voakes, 1998; Whitlow & Van Tubergen, 1978). Other important external influences that have been identified include informal groups with whom journalists work, the newsroom environment, competition, professional values, news subjects and sources, advertisers, and the audience (Breed, 1955; Singletary et al., 1990; Voakes, 1997; Weaver & Wilhoit, 1986, 1996; White & Pearce, 1991; White & Singletary, 1993). Another important influence on journalists' ethical decision making was motivation. Singletary and colleagues (1990; White & Singletary, 1993) developed and validated an Ethical Motivation Scale consistent with Kohlberg's stages. In these studies, external motivators such as those described previously were important, but intrinsic motivations proved to be more predictive of behavior. One of the ways to enhance individuals' reliance on intrinsic motivations is to increase their feelings of autonomy (Deci & Ryan, 1991). Autonomy is also a crucial variable in Kohlberg's (1981) theory; it is important for individuals to feel autonomous to attain the postconventional stage of moral development. McNeel's (1994) data suggest that choice, a construct related to autonomy, is important in moral growth.

Two other variables—investigative reporting and civic journalism—have been linked to moral development in journalists in qualitative literature only; this is a first attempt to test those ideas. Ettema and Glasser (1998; Glasser & Ettema, 1989) said that investigative reporters make moral decisions regarding what constitutes wrongdoing, and then abandon their objectivity to push for the public good. Peters and Cmiel (1991) noted that investigative journalists must serve as moral judges. Voakes (1998) confirmed that investigative reporting raised ethical issues more than did other types of reporting. Although no study has yet examined civic journalists' ethical orientations, many essays have linked it to communitarianism (Christians, Ferre, & Fackler, 1993; Hodges, 1996; Lambeth, 1992) and some have characterized it as a higher stage of moral development than is libertarianism (Glasser & Ettema, 1989; Peters & Cmiel, 1989). Before the rise of civic journalism, Culbertson (1983) studied activist journalists—to whom civic journalists have been likened—and found that activists bordered on Kohlberg's highest stage of moral development. Patterson and Hall (1998) linked the "common ground" rhetoric of civic journalism to the reasoning used by women at Gilligan's highest stage (1982).

Having briefly reviewed some of the DIT findings linked to demographic differences, we now turn to our sample of 249 journalists. As indicated in chapter 2, a representative sample was an appropriate research method for these particular scholarly questions. And, as also indicated in that chapter, it is appropriate ask whether the participants who constitute this representative sample "looked like" any other sample of journalists, but particularly one that employed random methodology.

Since the early 1970s, scholars (Johnstone et al., 1976; Weaver, Beam, Brownlee, Voakes, & Wilhoit, in press; Weaver and Wilhoit, 1986, 1996) have surveyed journalists about a variety of things. These studies, conducted once a decade, are now in their fourth iteration and provide a snapshot of the profession that is widely accepted as accurate in the way social scientists understand that term. Part of the reason for its wide acceptance is that the survey employs random methodology to collect the data. The most recent survey of 1,149 randomly selected U.S. journalists was completed in 2003 and was designed to match a universe of 116,000 editors, reporters, and producers working full time in the mainstream U.S. news media.

Table 3.1 provides a demographic comparison between this latest, random sample of journalists and the journalists who participated in the ethics test. Table 3.2 offers a geographic and medium comparison for those same groups of journalists. Although the groups of journalists surveyed are not identical demographically, it is clear that there is a close match between the two groups. Other characteristics of the DIT sample that are particularly pertinent for this study are as follows.

Education.   Because education has been linked to moral reasoning, the journalists who completed the DIT were asked some more specific

TABLE 3.1

Demographic Comparison Between DIT Survey and Weaver et al. (in press) Random Sample Survey of U.S. Journalists

	DIT Journalists	U.S. Journalists
Gender		
Men	62%	67%
Women	38%	33%
Race		
Caucasian	89%	90.5%
Of color	11%	9.5%
Education		
College graduates	92%	89%
Political Ideology		
Democrats	37.1%	42%
Republicans	18.6%	17%
Independents	33.5%	41%
Religion		
Protestant	36%	54.4%*
Catholic	29%	29.9%*
Jewish	4%	5.4%*
Other or none	31%	10.2%*

*Indicates data from the Weaver and Wilhoit (1996) survey.

TABLE 3.2

Geographic and Medium Comparison Between DIT Survey and Weaver et al. (in press) Random Sample Survey of U.S. Journalists

	DIT Journalists	U.S. Journalists
Medium		
Television	18%	14%
Print	82%	77%**
Geographic Region		
Northeast	20%	32%*
Midwest	25%	28%*
South	38%	32%*
West	17%	8%*

*Indicates data from the Weaver and Wilhoit (1996) survey. Data for 2004 not yet available.
**Does not total 100% because radio journalists were not included from the Weaver et al. (in press) study, as the DIT survey did not include radio.

questions about education than those reported by Weaver et al. (in press). In the DIT sample, 62% of the journalists had earned a bachelors degree, 13% had some graduate training, and an additional 17% had earned a graduate degree. Only 8% of those taking the DIT characterized themselves as having "some college or a high school degree." This level of educational attainment would suggest that this group of journalists would perform well on the DIT.

Professional Experience and Affiliation. The journalists who took the DIT averaged 38 years of age and 14 years in the profession. They were not novices. This descriptive characteristic parallels another of the Weaver et al.'s (in press) findings: The average age of journalists in that survey was older than in previous years, 41 years of age compared to 36 for the survey administered a decade earlier.

The journalists who took the DIT belonged to an average of just under one (.81) professional organization. They had attended an average of one seminar in the year before they completed the test.

The journalists who took the DIT also were asked about the kind of journalism they practice. Of all the journalists who completed the DIT, 28.5% said they had done some work in the past year that could be characterized as civic journalism, 7.2% said they had done some investigative reporting, and 46% said they had done both civic and investigative journalism. About 18% of the journalists who completed the DIT said they had done neither civic nor investigative work in the past year.

JOURNALISTS' ETHICAL REASONING

As indicated in the previous chapter, the DIT is based on Kohlberg's understanding of moral development. Our participants received four dilemmas from the DIT—a test that is copyrighted and hence cannot be reproduced here. The ethical issues participants confronted in those four problems were: Should Heinz steal the drug (a scenario outlined in chap. 1), a dilemma that focused on administrative censorship of a high school newspaper, a dilemma that asked whether a doctor should help a terminally ill patient to die, and a scenario that focused on whether an escaped prisoner should be reported to authorities after living an exemplary life for 8 years. These four scenarios have been part of the DIT since its inception.

To these scenarios we added two more designed to evaluate journalists' ethical reasoning in general and journalists' responses to visual information in particular. The original dilemmas demanded new issue statements. Many of these statements were taken from the DIT with only minor wording changes. Others were more specific to journalism, such as "Using unnamed sources is the only way to get the evidence this story needs." In all cases in which wording was modified or new statements were developed, statistical tests were conducted to make certain that the new statements correlated with several other statements used in the DIT to reflect a specific stage of moral reasoning while, at the same time, not correlating with statements from any other stage. The new dilemmas are reproduced as boxed text in this chapter and in the Appendix at the end of the book.

Given the literature on the DIT and on the influences on moral development in general, we expected that journalists' scores would equal those of many other professional groups that have taken the test in the past three decades. Because the P score is a cumulative measure of decisions on the scenarios, how journalists decided these questions also is important:

- On the four original DIT dilemmas, 54% said it was inappropriate for Heinz to steal the drug, 26% said stealing the drug was ethical, and 20% could not decide.
- On the dilemma involving physician-assisted suicide, 31% said the doctor should not help the patient die, 48% said the doctor should help, and 21% could not decide.

- In the dilemma about reporting the escaped prisoner, 50% said reporting was appropriate, 23% said reporting was not appropriate, and 27% could not decide.
- Finally, in responding to the journalistic dilemma about the newspaper, 82% of the journalists said the administrators should not censor the newspaper; only 9% said censorship was appropriate, and an equal percentage could not decide.
- Responses on the questions that asked journalists to think visually were as follows: 78% said using hidden cameras was appropriate, 12% said it was not, and 10% could not decide. In the case where the photograph was provided, 76% said it was appropriate to run the photo, 16% said the photo should not be run, and 8% could not decide.

The chart in Table 3.3 places the aggregate of these decisions, the P score, in the context of other professionals who have responded to the same questions. There are several ways to analyze journalists' ranking within this context. In a scholarly sense, it is first important to note that all of the professionals who rank above journalists on the test generally have much more formal education than the bachelor's degree that characterized the majority of the journalists in this sample. The same is true for dental students, who ranked slightly below journalists. Nurses with bachelors' degrees, the next group in the ranking, had as much formal educa-

---

PHOTO DILEMMA

Pete Stevens is one of your newspaper's best photographers. He has just returned from an area of town frequented by drug dealers and addicts. Pete has a compelling photo to go with a story on the effects of drugs on children. The photo shows two children, Maria, age 5, and her 3-year-old brother, Jorge, whose parents are addicts. The parents think their children don't see what they do, but as this photo shows, the children have playing "junkie" down to a detailed routine.

The photo was taken in a public alley, and Maria and Jorge's parents gave your photographer permission to take pictures of the children for publication. Since then, however, the children's grandmother has heard about the photo and called your newsroom to ask that you not run the photo. There are mixed opinions in the newsroom. You have the final say. What would you do?

tion as journalists. Thus, formal education appears to be influential in how professional groups score on the DIT; however, educational achievement certainly does not explain all the rankings.

TABLE 3.3

Mean *P* Scores of Various Professions

Seminarians/philosophers	65.1	Veterinary students	42.2
Medical students	50.2	Navy enlisted personnel	41.6
Practicing physicians	49.2	Orthopedic surgeons	41
Journalists	**48.68**	Adults in general	40
Dental students	47.6	Business professionals	38.13
Nurses	46.3	Accounting undergraduates	34.8
Lawyers	46	Accounting auditors	32.5
Graduate students	44.9	Business undergraduates	31.35
Undergraduate students	43.2	High school students	31
Pharmacy students	42.8	Prison inmates	23.7

HIDDEN CAMERAS

TV reporter Lauren Gray is investigating patient abuse by home health providers—private agencies that send health workers into homes to do everything from housecleaning to semi-skilled nursing. The Better Business Bureau has logged multiple complaints about patient abuse and so has the state nursing home board, but they lack authority to act. District Attorney Paul Johnson tells Gray that while his office has begun a criminal investigation, it has been stymied by a lack of evidence or by frail or elderly witnesses who may be unconvincing in court. Gray is urged to pursue the story, the officials involved agreeing to release public documents and go on the record.

Seven people receiving in-home care have agreed to let Gray place hidden cameras in their homes for a week so she can tape the care providers. Should wrongdoing occur, Gray plans to speak to the provider, show the tape and ask for an on-the-record response. If no wrongdoing occurs, Gray plans to report this as well. You are the executive producer who must decide whether to use the hidden cameras. What would you do?

Second, it is important to note that there was a dilemma focusing specifically on medicine in the original DIT, just as there was a journalistic scenario. Research indicates that people can be expected to do better ethical thinking within an area of life—what psychologists call a *domain*—with which they are familiar. In this sense, journalists had no greater advantage on the DIT than did various sorts of medical professionals, some of whom scored higher and others of whom scored lower on the test. When evaluated in this way, journalists appear capable of the same level of ethical thinking that society expects from other professionals with significant domain expertise and formal academic training.

There is some irony is this result. Public opinion would not support such an assessment. In fact, in a frequently cited poll of professional trustworthiness, in terms of ethics the American public ranks journalists above only used car salespersons.

However, aggregate scores can explain only so much and, based on the literature, it was important to examine the results from other perspectives. The journalists' DIT scores followed the larger literature in some important ways.

Gender.   There was no statistically significant difference in the scores of male journalists (mean P score $= 48.7$, $SD = 12.5$) and female journalists (mean P score $= 48.6$, $SD = 13$). The literature predicts this result.

Professional Environment.   There was no statistically significant difference between broadcast journalists (mean P score $= 47.9$, $SD = 12$) and print journalists (mean P score $= 48.9$, $SD = 13$). This lack of significant difference is explored in more depth later in this book, but what is important to note here is that the consistency of the results across mediums is somewhat counter to traditional thinking about these two wings of the same profession.

Managerial Role.   Similar results emerged for managers. If the term *manager* was defined as a person who had the power to "hire and fire" in the news organization, about 90% of the journalists who took the DIT were in nonmanagement positions. If, on the other hand, the definition of *manager* was expanded to encompass those who had some capacity to make final decisions about news content, then about 31% of the journalists in the DIT cohort exercised this sort of management function. Regardless of the particular management role the journalists played, there was no statistically significant difference in P scores between managers and nonmanagers. This result certainly runs counter to professional folk wisdom, which tends to blame management for all ills. (Top managers' mean P score = 48.79, SD = 13.4; midmanagers' mean P score = 48.8, SD = 12.3; nonmanagers' mean P score = 48.9, SD = 12.4).

Type of Journalism.   Although the level that a journalist had reached in the organization didn't matter in terms of ethical reasoning scores, the type of journalism these journalists produced did correlate with moral reasoning. Specifically, journalists who said they had done investigative journalism (mean P score = 55.28, SD = 12), both investigative reporting and civic journalism (mean P score = 49.65, SD = 12.2), and civic journalism (mean P score = 47.32, SD = 12.6) scored statistically significantly higher than did journalists who said their professional lives did not include either form of journalism (mean P score = 45.7, SD = 13.2). Previous studies, particularly of investigative reporters (Ettema & Glasser, 1998), indicated that investigative reporting entails making moral judgments and that the journalists who do this sort of work wrestle with ethical issues as a part of the reporting process. Similarly, civic journalism—particularly the institutional role that civic journalists sometimes play—has been the focus of both professional and scholarly reflection on its ethical implications. This correlational study cannot determine whether these forms of reporting help create better ethical reasoning, or if the journalists practicing them already possess that ability. It makes some sense that journalists whose professional work foregrounds ethical thinking would outscore other professionals whose work focuses on ethics in a more episodic way. After all, they are exercising their ethical muscles on a more regular basis. This analysis is supported, in part, by the findings in *Good Work* (Gardner, Csikszentmihalyi, & Damon, 2001), which linked excellent professional performance with quality ethical thinking.

The element of practice—what scholars call *domain expertise*—was also reflected another way in the aggregate score. The journalists who took the DIT had mean P scores of 46.56 on the four original DIT dilemmas (SD = 15.2). The two journalistic dilemmas that were added to the test yielded a mean P score of 59.9 (SD = 17.4), a result that is statistically significant at a very high level. (t = −4.85, df = 248, p < .001).

Finally, aggregates and averages are just that—they find a mathematical middle ground between extremes. What they do not reflect is individual variation in scoring, something that any statistician would expect and something that also was reflected in the P scores for the journalists.

On one end of the continuum—what philosophers might call the ethically challenged end—2.7% of the journalists who took the DIT scored below 24—the average P score for prison inmates. About 9.3% of the journalists scored 31 or below—the average score for high school students. Approximately 24.9% of the journalists who responded scored below 40—the average for all adults. Again, these results seem reasonable, particularly because education is highly correlated with P scores and individual variation is to be expected in any population. It is certainly reasonable to expect that the majority of the journalists—in this case, about 75% of them—would score at levels equal to or greater than those of average American adults.

On the other end of the continuum—the one that philosophers might suggest reflect people of considerable moral wisdom—11% of the journalists (a total of 27) compiled a P score of 65 or above. Again, although individual variation is to be expected, it is appropriate to note that many journalists, as evidenced by the results of the DIT, were good ethical thinkers in general and particularly good ethical thinkers about questions dealing with their professional work. Those who assert that, as a profession, individual journalists are somehow morally handicapped should not take much comfort from this result.

Finally, a regression model was developed in an effort to see if it was possible to predict DIT scores based on other elements in journalists' lives. The responses to the questions at the end of the survey asked participants everything from political and religious affiliation, to the type of journalistic work conducted, to motivations and autonomy on the job. These responses were grouped into four factors that appeared to have some influence on P scores. These factors explain about 15% of the total variation in participants' P scores. This level of explanation of variance is considered acceptable in the social sciences, although it would drive a chemist or physicist back to the laboratory in despair.

Five factors emerged, three of which helped explain the P scores. The first factor was titled *religion*, and just as religion has in other studies, this factor was significantly and negatively correlated to journalists' P scores. In other words, those who said they placed less emphasis on religion in their lives were statistically more likely to get a higher P score than were those who said they placed more importance on religion.

The second factor, called *rules and law*, combined responses about how the participants viewed the law and employer-generated guidelines and rules. This factor also was significantly and negatively correlated with higher P scores. Those journalists who said they placed less importance on laws and specific employer regulations and policies tended to score higher on the DIT. Again, this finding makes sense if moral development theory is correct. As people—in this case, journalists—begin to internalize the reasons behind the rules, rule-based obedience gives way to more principled and universal ethical thinking. Just as in the case of religion, it was not that rules were discounted entirely; rather, they were balanced with other elements that the journalists believed to be important in making the appropriate decision.

The third important factor, titled *internal environment*, was significantly and positively correlated with higher *P* scores. The internal environment included elements such as a journalists' sense of right and wrong, a commitment to ethical principles, and the public's right to know. This internal factor may provide some insight into the mechanism that allows journalists to respond appropriately in ethical dilemmas; they believe they have the capacity to know right from wrong and the professional self-confidence to act on these understandings. This internal moral center certainly reflects Erikson's notion of adult development: Journalists who have successfully negotiated professional demands and opportunities and internalized those understandings are able to act on them in many different situations.

Two other important variables emerged; one was *choice*.

Journalists who had more choice—about the kind of stories they covered and the type of journalism they did—were significantly more likely to have higher *P* scores than were journalists who said they had less choice. Doing investigative reporting, which is often a career or assignment choice for journalists and which involves making many other sorts of decisions (among them story topic, approach, etc.), also predicted higher *P* scores. Again, this finding fits well with general moral development theory—choosing often means findings reasons for choices—a process that is at the core of ethical reasoning. Investigative reporting, because the work is often quite analytic and is seldom the purview of novices, should aid in the development of such critical thinking skills.

There also were some factors and variables that appeared to have little to no influence on *P* scores. The fact that gender did not have an effect in the regression analysis merely provides more rigorous statistical support to a general finding in the literature. The external environment factor with the exception of the issues surrounding choice, also did not appear to exert much influence. This external environment factor referred to influences outside the journalists themselves, such as how colleagues would handle the story. This finding also applied to working in a competitive media market, something for which the qualitative comments reviewed in the next chapter provide some support. Additionally, age was not a good predictor of *P* scores—a result that is probably subsumed by the influence of education, which to some extent also reflects age, at least through the graduate education process. Table 3.4 provides the mathematical results of the regression for those who wish to examine them more closely.

CONCLUSIONS: HOW TO BUILD BETTER JOURNALISTS

Professionals can take heart in these findings. Journalists as a profession appear to be strong ethical thinkers, although there is some variation among individuals in that ability. Education clearly matters, and, as the demographics indicate, journalists as a profession are slowly becoming better educated. Part of that education—whether it is formal or more job based—indicates there is a journalistic domain of knowledge and that journalists think even better about the ethical problems connected with that domain than they do about ethics in general. Give journalists a choice in the sort of professional work they attempt, expose them to the rigors of investigative reporting, moderate the influence of work-based rules and religion, and journalists are capable of high-level ethical thinking.

Psychologists examining these results also should take heart. Much in these findings confirms the general outlines of moral development theory and some of the specific findings in scholarly research (e.g., the effect of gender). In addition, these findings suggest that visual information certainly does not impede moral thinking and, in fact, in certain circumstances may enhance it. Just how that process works is the subject of chapter 5. However, statistics can only reveal so much. In order to understand the nuances of reasoning, a more qualitative approach was also employed. That is the focus of the next chapter.

TABLE 3.4

Unstandardized and Standardized Regression Coefficients for Variables Predicting Moral Development in Journalists

	Model 1		Model 2		Model 3	
	B (SE)	Beta B	B (SE)	Beta B	B (SE)	Beta B
Intercept	43.1(4.9)***		36.6(8.67)***		28.8(8.83)***	
Gender (male = 1)	.84 (1.7)	.032	.73 (1.6).	.028	1.27 (1.6)	.05
Age	–.09 (.08)	–.076	–.07 (.08)	–.06	–.11 (.08)	–.09
Education	1.96 (.94)*	.134	1.56 (.9)	.11	1.6 (.88)	.11
External environment			–.27 (.93)	–.022	–.76 (.92)	–.06
Religion			–1.77 (.45)***	–.24	–1.7 (.44)***	–.24
Rules and law			–1.8 (.85)*	–.15	–1.8 (.83)*	–1.6
Competition			–.51 (.54)	–.06	–.56 (.53)	–.07
Internal environment			3.97 (1.2)**	.21	3.6 (1.2)**	–.19
Choice					.5 (.25)*	.13
Investigative reporting					.7 (.27)**	.16
Civic J					–.08	.26
R^2	.008		.10***		.15***	

*$p < .05$; **$p < .01$; ***$p < .001$; Nearly significant, $p = .06$

45

CHAPTER 4

Moral Development: In Their Own Words

Psychologists like paper-and-pencil tests because they force participants to chose among alternatives. Scholars can then analyze what seems to influence what appear to be discrete and disconnected choices according to a variety of other criteria. However, although supporting this sort of analytic and compartmentalized approach, paper-and-pencil tests omit something at least as crucial—the subtlety of human thought. In addition, ethical thinking demands an understanding of nuance and shades of meaning as well as logical analysis. We didn't want to lose the nuance of journalistic thought in deference to analytic rigor, so we provided the participants who took the DIT with a space to explain their choices. Many studies employ this combination of quantitative and qualitative approaches to data collection but discover that participants seldom write much, even when provided the opportunity. Such was not the case here. One indication that the instrument worked was that almost all those who took the DIT made the effort to provide a more detailed explanation of their thinking. Analyzing these qualitative responses revealed the subtleties—as well as the development—of journalists' ethical reasoning.

THINKING ABOUT HIDDEN CAMERAS: LEGALITY, ROLE, AND ENDS

Hidden cameras have been contentious in journalistic practice since their first use almost a century ago. As ethicists view it, hidden cameras represent one point in a continuum of deceptive newsgathering techniques (which are reviewed and analyzed in more detail in chap. 7). Recent professional history has also reinforced the troubling elements of this newsgathering approach that, on its face, seems ethically problematic. Perhaps the most publicized event in recent professional history is the now notorious Food Lion case, although the notoriety of the case almost certainly means different things to different people. To audience members, Food Lion represents a victory for those who find the act of "spying" to get a story reprehensible—a public rebuke of a profession that will seemingly do anything, including trampling on the rights and privacy of others, to get a story. To journalists, Food Lion represents a far different issue, the intrusion of the legal system into information collection and storytelling that ultimately ruled in favor of process—no hidden cameras, no working undercover—while marginalizing truthtelling about grocery stores selling tainted meat, a genuine public health hazard. Yet, despite the Food Lion verdict, hidden cameras remain a staple of reporting, especially on television news, where they become particularly prominent during sweeps, and on evening primetime magazine shows that must compete with entertainment offerings for viewers.

Given this history and professional context, it is reasonable that some of the DIT respondents said their decision about hidden cameras was grounded in what the law would allow. Some journalists wrote:

> I would thoroughly investigate state laws ands cases like *Food Lion* to see if there were problems of which I'm unaware.

> I'm not sure it's legal. I would get the opinion of numerous lawyers before deciding to tape even an in-house caretaker without their knowledge. If it's all right, I'll go ahead. I'd be concerned about lawsuits.

> If an attorney advised it was legal to use the cameras, it would be the best way to get the story.

> The biggest factor is legality. Chances are this place is private and one would need its consent, as in the *Food Lion* case. The question: Can we do this story and find this information / evidence in some other way?

A distinct minority, fewer than 10% of the more than 200 written comments about the hidden camera scenario, focused on legality, what Kohlberg and the DIT both classified as the conventional ethical reasoning that characterizes thinking in the third and fourth stages. Ethicists say it somewhat differently. This line of thinking is generally characterized as ethical legalism, meaning it is ethical to do what the law allows—generally considered a minimalist approach to ethical thinking. The most critical analysis of ethical legalism is that decision making done in this way requires little independent thought, merely a following of the legal rules. Additionally, ethical legalism certainly provides no intellectual mechanism for

understanding the "reason for the rules" that Piaget and others characterized as the hallmark of sophistical ethical reasoning. This rule-based approach was reflected in another comment:

> Gannett has an ethics policy that prohibits such tactics. They tell report-
> ers to find another way to get the story or don't do the story.

The more expansive view is that much law is founded in both ethical theory and ethical thinking about how people should relate to one another.
Viewed in this light, the law provides a sort of ethical shorthand—a quick
way of reaching a decision that is not less deep merely because it has been
codified.

The participants in this study clearly saw the law as being connected to
other issues:

> I'm assuming the use is legal in that state. The reporter appeared to have
> cooperation from authorities. If it's a "he said/she said" case—this may
> be the only way to obtain evidence. Helpless people could be victim-
> ized—someone should uncover that.

In particular, the respondents were concerned about the privacy of both
the elderly people who were being cared for and the health care workers
themselves, arguably two of the most central stakeholders in this scenario.
Two journalists noted:

> The home owners approved the camera, so you are not trespassing. You
> are not invading the home owners' privacy either—you have their per-
> mission.

> With the permission of those receiving care, I believe it is not deceptive.
> The problem would be it the elderly person either did not know about
> the taping or did not give permission. The elderly person must also have
> [his or her] mental faculties.

In a comment that can apply both to those who are receiving care—the
victims in this story—as well as to those who are providing it; a third journalist wrote:

> The invasions of privacy can be mitigated by interviews or prior con-
> sent. If the person who runs the home gave permission, there was no
> breach of trust. You cannot expect privacy outside of your own private
> space.

Other participants addressed the idea that the privacy of the victims should outweigh that of the health care providers:

> Home owners agreed to allow cameras; [it] was the only way to secure information needed; safety of elderly clients transcends privacy right[s] of [the] vendor; those not mistreating have nothing to fear.

> The key question is where the cameras were set up. It was on the property of people who gave permission, so that's key. That makes it legal. The issue still is clearly important, if the healthcare providers would be given a complete chance to respond.

> [This is] no different [than] the reporter who leaves his tape recorder in a room or the reporter who asks what was said when he wasn't there. And, this is on private property with consent of the property owner. The ethical question enters with the hidden camera and mixes entering private property without consent of owner or police if they've seized the property without warrant.

At least one other participant could not come to the same conclusions when weighing the same issues, writing:

> I couldn't make a decision because the right to privacy for the good caregivers was such an important issue for me. I had trouble making the leap to the "end justifies the means."

These comments and many others like them demonstrated that participants negotiated among multiple ethical principles when arriving at a decision.

Moral development theory has been of two minds on how two interpret such a weighing process. Scholars in the Piaget, Erikson, and Kohlberg traditions placed emphasis on ultimate choices and using those choices as a mechanism to gauge moral development. Scholars who take the approach of Carol Gilligan in psychology and feminist theorists in philosophy would interpret the same balancing process differently. They would argue that the sense of connection—between the caregivers and the providers and between the journalists and the audience—is crucial to making an appropriate choice. These responses seem to reflect the ethics of care and connection at least as much as the ethics of rights and responsibilities.

Thinking About Ethics Involves Process

One strategy the participants in the DIT study said they used to decide among competing ethical alternatives was to rely on good journalistic process—what many referred to as a *best practices approach* to the situation. Moral development theory is essentially silent on such an approach; the approach clearly smacks of rule following but also requires some creativity and adaptation to particular situations. Classical ethical theory—particularly the work of Aristotle, McIntyre, and other virtue ethicists—maintains that adherence and application of best practices reflects distilled professional wisdom and the character to employ it. Such an approach, this thinking would suggest, would be the mark of a moral adult. In Kohlberg's and Rest's views, this level of moral thought probably characterizes thinking at the fourth stage—and, indeed, the majority of participant comments focused on issues of journalistic process as a means to a particular end.

The means troubled many of the participants:

> A hidden camera captures everything—it's sort of a video fishing expedition that violates a person's expectation of privacy. Public records and interviews tell the story, though perhaps not as dramatically.

> Hidden camera make me leery. It's almost as if you're becoming part of the story—that's not right.

> The story would not need hidden cameras to be successful.

A similar response was given in more detail—again with a reference to best practices—by another participant:

> Hidden cameras do not win popularity contests or ethical sweepstakes. However, when people are succumbing to a bad system or bad people within that system, we ought to show it. Otherwise, perhaps nothing would be done. However, there are alternatives; consider Katherine Boo's masterful investigation of privately run D.C. group homes for the mentally retarded. That used documents and interviews, no hidden cameras.

However, some journalists were not willing to reject the technique out of hand:

> Just because of *Food Lion* we can't stop uncovering these "hidden" stories.

> This was the only way to get a story that very much needed to be told.

Those who opted for the cameras were careful to note that the cameras had to be used to show multiple elements of the story:

This was the only thing to do. The patient's right to receive care outweighs the abusers' right to privacy. Everyone given the opportunity to respond and both sides of the story reported. Making a criminal case viable has nothing to do with it.

[I'm in favor of hidden cameras] because two reasons: First, the elderly subjects gave permission for their homes to be videotaped. Second, the reporter promises to air the results no matter the outcome—that's responsible journalism, not sensationalism. Lawsuits may occur, but if abuse is witnessed and stopped, then a greater good has been done.

This element of presenting both sides—those of workers who did and those of workers who did not abuse patients—was important:

In using a hidden camera, I would not use one unless it was presented to both parties. It is important to show evidence in these cases, however both sides need to be represented. Using the cameras brings it into full view.

Other journalists noted:

[T]o not report/cover a story like those would be irresponsible. The cameras are the necessary component for showing a societal ill. The fact both good and bad behavior would be reported and that those behaving poorly have a chance to respond, I believe it was fairly approached.

... it was the only way to get the evidence. We had the patient's permission, and we would get response from any caregivers shown to have caused harm. This case involves people being physically hurt—otherwise, I wouldn't do it or allow a hidden camera. This was an exceptional case.

Again, we are telling a story. But in this case we are also allowing both sides a chance at discussion after the hidden cameras are used. If nothing happens, there is an opportunity to say that the allegations are false and the district attorney has a chance to respond with his course of action. If it does, the people involved are given the opportunity to discuss why. As long as the report is fair, hidden cameras are a journalist's tool in this instance.

A participant crystallized the competing ethical claims this way:

This one [the scenario] was more difficult than photo because hidden cameras are a dangerous tool if misused. But, I wouldn't think of another way to prove the abuse. And, society benefits by knowing. And the providers would be given ample time for a response. So, I would use in this case.

These same issues were broached by another participant in different words:

> Journalists are taught that we should never use deception to get a story. Rules, however, are made to be broken, and in this case, the public was better served learning about this issue. My greatest issue would be fairness and objectivity. It would be easy to exploit a video like this one.

However, even where there was a balancing act at work, no journalist who took the DIT said that the story was not newsworthy or that it failed to capture an important issue facing an aging society. Comments included:

> This is a serious problem of which I have first-hand knowledge. I don't know of another way to get that information.

> Abuse of elderly or children needs to be exposed and stopped.

Sentiments with overtones of journalistic duty were expressed by many respondents:

> It will show how the system failed.

> It will serve as the voice of the elderly who are being abused.

More than one journalist was willing to face possible legal action in the case:

> If defenseless elderly people are truly being abused, the opportunity to end such abuse should not be thrown aside over possible legal action.

> I'm not a fan of hidden cameras, but this story and the benefit to the public good warrants their use.

Several journalists accepted that the story could bring about change. For them, change was a goal of such reporting:

> It would bring about positive change.

> [Cameras are appropriate] to help draw attention to a problem in real life examples so society can correct (or try to).

Some journalists articulated this potential for change in concrete objectives:

> The helpless elderly need protection from abusers, and this exposure could help.

[This approach] possibly prevents serious harm or death to these and other patients.

It would save people's lives. It could help clean up a messy system. It could definitely show the abuse or lack of. People might not tell you the same things a camera would show. I am still shocked by the *Food Lion* decision.

Hidden cameras seemed the only way to expose serious, frightening abuse of vulnerable community and I don't think those people should be abused and would want [me] to do whatever I can to put a stop to it.

These comments indicate that the journalists not only "imagined" the plight of the elderly stakeholders in the case, but also saw the societywide implications. Again, theories of moral development suggest that, on the route to higher-level thinking, ethical principles themselves must become internalized and universalized. These responses make clear that many participants who took the DIT saw the wider implications—for some groups of stakeholders— of the case and were willing, even eager, to use a variety of reporting techniques to fulfill the journalistic role of truthteller. Even those participants who objected to the hidden cameras often suggested ways to "get the story" without them. It is a reasonable inference that such suggestions would be made only if the participants believe the story needed to be told.

Although the journalistic role of truthteller was a predominant response for those who focused their comments on the outcome of such reporting, for a minority there was an element of "gotcha" journalism involved in the decision. Phrased in more philosophical terms, these journalists suggested that in this case lying to liars was justifiable:

Apparently in this case, the hidden camera could make the difference in whether a criminal is caught. If the reporter can help get a criminal off the street and alert the public to a dangerous situation, the society benefits.

If we can prevent criminal activity, we should.

It appears the only means left to capture proof of abuse. If home-case recipients agreed, go for it.

[Such techniques are acceptable] because abusing the elderly is a widespread problem that needs to be addressed. Also, those who take advantage of the elderly should be dealt with in a harsh manner.

Others noted that the hidden camera, in some sense, relies on the bad actions of others to make its case. If caregivers in the scenario treated patients well, then they had nothing to fear from the reporting:

In this case, you don't have a story without the evidence. I don't think it's unfair or would damage the assailant's chance at a fair trial. No one made him/her strike or abuse the elderly person.

The permission of the elderly involved was given. Those violating the law would be the only ones harmed.

It was the best way to prove abuse, and if none occurred, it showed people with good records.

Hidden cameras would allow the "true" story to be told—whether there was abuse or not.

Some participants were sensitive to the fact that viewers might perceive the approach as lazy or a form of ambush journalism:

> If there was no better way to document abuse cases, I would approve the use of hidden cameras. It is critical to both report those instances where no abuse was filmed, and to give spokespeople for the companies an opportunity to respond on camera—otherwise it has the look of ambush journalism. Because the issue of abuse of the ill and elderly is an important one (if, as in this case, there are numerous reports of such), it's an issue worth investigating.

Although some participants wanted to function as change agents through their reporting, others shied away from the implication that such a story might bring about change:

> Hidden cameras don't bother me. It isn't for newspaper to make cases for prosecution, only to present information to its readers/viewers.

This comment and others like it reflect the tension that journalists feel between their role as neutral arbiters of fact and the implications of such reporting on public opinion and policy.

Thinking About Universals Supported Two Distinct Choices

Finally, about 25% of those who commented wrote statements that could be characterized as reflecting the implementation of universal principles. Significantly, the majority of those who opposed using hidden cameras provided these sorts of statements. However, a substantial minority of those who chose to employ hidden cameras for the story also linked their decisions to one or more of the universal principles of classical ethical philosophy.

Among those who decided against hidden cameras:

We have so many problems as a profession that I don't think we can risk even the perception of ethical problems.

Being up-front is important.

This was a tough call. Generally speaking, I think journalists should be above the law in pursuing stories and not resort to deception.

Journalists should not deceive to get the news.

[I] don't believe it's ethical to place hidden cameras in someone's home.

[This practice] lessens credibility with stories that follow.

I believe that people have the right to be free from surveillance and that this outweigh the benefits to be gained from gathering the evidence.

Honesty is the best policy, especially when there are other ways to achieve your newsgathering goals: Do things to increase the elderly people's credibility.

I just think hidden cameras are deceptive and could cause more problems then they are worth.

It would require an extraordinary reason (e.g., terrorist investigation) to deliberately jeopardize the rights of others.

Using hidden cameras is unethical, and doing something this wrong would hurt the news operation's reputation more than anything gained from doing the story.

[I] would prefer to try and get the story without resorting to deceptive practices—which may cast doubt because of the unsavory way information was gathered.

Among those who favored using the technique in this instance:

Once again, we are talking about those who have placed the care and trust in others. When those "others" compromise trust, it needs to be reported.

The system has failed the vulnerable people. The media have a duty to pursue the story.

The truth is a powerful and often frightening thing, but is absolutely essential to improve society.

Balancing rights: What is the greater good? A key for me: The cameras are in patients' homes; they make the call on allowing them. This whole approach, though, makes me queasy; we should not allow our reports to deceive.

Only truth can solve problems—period. Sanitized news helps nothing.

The deception in this case was necessary to uncover a potential crime against a very helpless part of society.

Information that is accurate is essential for an electorate to make decisions as to how they will deal with problems in their community.

Was this the only way to get the truth? Seems like it.

The camera could prove the story to be true or false. It doesn't benefit one side or the other, only the truth.

In general, the responses summarized here do not always fit neatly into particular stages of moral development. Whereas some clearly edge more toward conventional thinking and hence imply a somewhat lower level of development, and others appear more universal and hence imply a higher level.

Another factor that is probably at least as significant is the number of issues the journalists evaluated before making their decisions. Furthermore, complex thinking incorporates elements—duty, character, and veracity— that classical philosophers would recognize. Some, but a minority, took a very Kantian perspective—never lie. This is a universal ethical principle that all would recognize, although even in the rarified fields of philosophy Kant's maxim has generated enormous debate. Others universalized the notion of "tell the truth," another and more difficult rendering of Kant's maxims as well as a foundational principle of journalism. Still others balanced competing duties, such as those reflected in the writings of W. D. Ross (1930): Treat others with dignity, give back to a society that has given much to you, speak for the powerless, and be a good steward of both your profession and the lives of those around you. All of these notions reflect high-level ethical thinking, but in a way that logic based on what is "right" only incompletely acknowledges.

What became clear in this case was that the participants were not moral midgets. They understood both rights and responsibilities. And, as the responses to the "junkie kids" photo indicated, they wrestled with the implications of connection as well.

SEEING CONNECTIONS:
CHILDREN, EMOTION, AND JOURNALISTIC ENDS

The levels of reasoning represented in the open-ended responses to the second visual dilemma did not differ markedly from the responses about hidden cameras. However, the responses themselves did differ in at least two significant ways. First, the photograph provided a view of one set of stakeholders—an element of moral reasoning that was articulated concretely and repeatedly in the open-ended comments. Journalists, who are trained to use nouns rather than abstract concepts in their writing, used one noun more than any other in explaining their reasoning: the *children*. Second, these responses emphasized connection in a way that the slightly more abstract responses to the hidden camera scenario did not.

There was one universal in this set of responses: None of the participants said that the photograph itself was poor or of unpublishable quality. In fact, quite the opposite—participants founds the photo disturbing and moving. It evoked an emotional response:

> ... because it gives a strong and compelling portrait of what drug use by parents can do to children. Because printing it illustrated the extent of the problem, it's a picture you'll never forget.

Words that summoned emotions were common in the journalists' analysis of the photo. Theoretically, this is important. Emotion is often an indicator that a viewer paid close attention, and research shows that paying close attention indicates central route processing in the brain. The fact that emotion appeared to be part of many of the responses thus indicates that journalists gave the ethical issue serious reflection—which should, in turn, be detectable in the P score for this particular dilemma. As chapter 3 indicated, the average P score for this scenario was the second highest for any dilemma. The open-ended responses reveal one reason—emotion and ensuing central route processing—which supports a P score that denotes able moral thinking.

The universal acceptance of the journalistic value of the photograph is important for another reason. One of the most common responses working journalists provide to questions involving photographs center around craft norms—in other words, is the photograph itself technically adequate (exposed properly, framed well, etc.) and aesthetically standard. Often, journalists will reject a photograph for craft reasons, saying that it is of poor quality. Ethics doesn't enter into the discussion. Similarly, journalists may accept a photograph because it's a "great shot." Here again, craft overwhelms other sorts of analysis. The "junkie kids" photograph had been carefully selected to try to mitigate those responses, and the open-ended responses to the scenario indicated overwhelmingly that ethics—not craft—was the central focus of journalistic analysis.

The most common craft-related response the participants gave was that the photograph "furthered" the story in important ways:

> … because I assumed the story was as strong as the photo, increasing the impact of the piece. If the story didn't live up to the photo, I'd kill the photo.

However, these craft considerations—which were somewhat rare in the more than 200 written responses to the scenario—were almost always linked to other, more ethical, considerations:

> It is a compelling photo made in a public place and with permission— and it truly helps tell the story.

> It was factual, accurate, and a part of society that exists.

> It's real and it perfectly illustrates the story and the horrors of drug abuse and the effect it has on children.

> It demonstrates the story.

Just as in the responses to the hidden camera scenario, 10% of the journalists said they based their ethical thinking on what they knew the law would allow:

> The photo makes it real. It happened, you can't show the same things with words.

> Plus, the photographer had the family's permission in advance. The family shouldn't be able to back out just because something had happened.

> The parents gave their permission to print the photo, and the photo emphasizes just how terribly children are impacted by drugs.

For this group of journalists, the fact that parental permission had been obtained to take the photo and the fact that the photo had been shot in a public place was critical. These journalist knew that the U.S. Supreme Court has ruled that what takes place in a public place cannot be considered, in any legal sense, private behavior protected by the admittedly difficult and often contradictory legal rulings about the issue. Parental permission to photograph minors also negates legal culpability under the American system of jurisprudence. This legal foundation was important, and for one group of journalists, it was the central factor in their decision:

> It graphically shows what can happen to children who grow up in a world of narcotics. We had the permission of the parents to take it.

Permission is key. Had the photo been taken without permission, especially had the children not been [in] a public easement, I would at least have shrouded their identities. But with permission, showing their faces best shows the truth of it.

If the parent[s] were so far gone that they felt they had nothing to hide—allowing a photographer to shoot their kids—then journalists should feel free to run it.

Ethical legalism—following the rules—certainly dominated these answers. However, many of the answers that were framed in law also summoned other ethical concepts, particularly truthtelling, as the previous two quotes indicate, plus the larger social good. Another respondent commented:

The photo was taken in a public place, the parents were aware of it, and gave permission to use it. Benefits to society seem to outweigh concerns about the effect on the people involved.

STAKEHOLDERS MOVE TO THE FOREGROUND OF THOUGHT

Although previous scholarship indicates that following the rules—conventional thinking—is at the midrange of moral development, the participants' responses to the dilemma make it clear that there was an ethical reason, rather than a legal one, for giving strong consideration to "the rules." That reason focused on the stakeholders, and the stakeholders about whom participants were most concerned were the children of the drug-addicted parents. Furthermore, reasoning that focused on the stakeholders allowed journalists to come to two distinctly different conclusions about running the photograph. For a little less than half of those who focused on stakeholders in their comments, the effect on the children outweighed all other considerations:

People are saturated with negativity on the news and in newspaper all the time. Sometime words could describe the situation just as well without using the picture. The picture would seem to be exploiting the children.

[The] photo, for some, would glorify the behavior. I'm not interested in publishing "how to" material encouraging drug abuse among children.

Perhaps I was swayed by my former job as a DARE officer. I feel we have a duty to protect kids at any cost.

Problems of drug abuse are important and need to be discussed, but the children need to be protected. By publishing the picture you would "mark" them. There are better ways.

[I would not publish the photo] because the children are children. It would hold them up to public ridicule they do not deserve.

Many journalists believed running the photo would have a lasting impact:

I would not run a photo that could stigmatize the children for years, if not forever.

But others, who also centered their thinking on the stakeholders, concluded differently:

It was the right thing to do. What's ahead for the children? Death?

Running the photo might save them and other children.

While the photo would be painful for the family, I think it's something that should be seen. I think it's a very telling shot that shines a harsh light on the problem.

Some of these conclusions were reached only after real struggle:

It illustrates dramatically the effect [that] parent drug use has on the children. I am torn, however, over the issue of whether an innocent child should be exposed this way probably knowing he or she may suffer for it in the future.

This was tough—back and forth. Finally, [I] decided kids were minors who had to be protected. They did not give consent. Also, [I] doubt [the] parents would if the children knew subject of the photo.

For just a few, the competing claims were so nearly balanced that indecision resulted:

I can't decide—my biggest worry is the future impact on these two children—should this photo [the handwriting here was illegible] them all their lives. To hell with their parents.

However, the majority of the journalists who articulated thoughts that centered on stakeholders "saw" the issue this way:

Photos like this take the place of words and say more than paragraphs ever could. Some stories need to be shared—the effect parents' behavior has on kids is one of them. Striking images like this one are the kind that need to be shared.

It would awaken other druggie parents to the reality. [I] didn't think little kids would understand what they saw on the pix, and if older kids did understand what was happening, it would be a good time for parents to talk to their children about drugs.

These children are very young. They and many others are at great risk.

I don't like "the public has a right to know" language, but I think public understanding goes a long way toward creating solutions. It's shocking, but it's real. Public shock and horror can be creative forces. [A] parent's permission is key to the decision.

While it's a shocking photo, its impact would be great. If the grandmother isn't the primary guardian, she has little right to affect the photo unless she was, in fact, taking care of the children. The photo shows how drugs affect those around the addicts in a startling way. Its publication won't scare the kids; growing up in that environment will do that.

The children are in danger if they live in conditions like these. Their parents did give permission, however the example did not indicate if they were high at the time. People can benefit from a graphic example of how drug use damages more than just the user.

Journalists who reasoned in this way thought of their readers as potential actors on the issue:

The image is stronger than the words in the story. It creates a bridge to the reader and makes it a reality that must be confronted. I'd have a few questions about how the photo was obtained before I'd agree to run it, however.

Some journalists also said they believed it was significant that the photo itself might have an effect on the family:

It is reality. It is a story / photo obtained legally and fairly. And, it is an image that will stay with people. It drives home the point about kids and drugs. (And maybe social services will finally take action and get the kids' parents some help.)

It is a story that must be told. A picture is worth a thousand words and perhaps a thousand lives saved.

I feel, in this case, the welfare of the children in this photo is more important issue. And I think if the parents are part of the story, then that is
enough to get the "authorities" involved.

I think for as much impact as that photo could have one day on the parents, it would impact the children's lives for the rest of their lives—the
people having that photo, our readers, would not be the ones to change
drug abuse in children. The ones empowered to do so—the parents and
the DYS (social services)—already know the problem is out there and are
trying to rectify it. The photo does not shock anyone but those not in a
position to help.

The responses that focused on stakeholders are noteworthy for two
reasons. First, and unlike the responses to the hidden camera scenario,
many were emotional. Words like *shock* and *horror* were part of these responses, as were *drama* and *suffering*. The photo that was part of the dilemma clearly injected an emotional component into the reasoning
process. Also, it should be noted that journalists—perhaps more than
their readers or viewers—are accustomed to seeing and making decisions about emotion-laden images.

Second, the responses that centered on stakeholders also revealed the
sense of connection that the participants felt toward both the subjects of
the story—primarily the children—and their readers. Kohlberg's descrip-
tion of moral development does not neatly account for the ethical import
of connectedness. However, this notion can be explained by the insights
of Carol Gilligan and others who have argued that the ethics of care constitutes a differently understood but equally mature understanding of
moral development. Connection provided the participants with a reason
to run the photo (the dominant decision) and to withhold it (due primarily to privacy and considerations of long-term harm). Both "final" decisions were based in ethical theory, yet called on connection as an
additional element with moral weight. For these participants, that moral
weight also spoke to the potential impact of the photo, and hence to journalistic role and the impact of publicity. Although most respondents said
the photo would spur thought and action on the part of readers, others
said that the information contained in the photo and story would also
cause those in political power—who could have some specific impact on
this particular case—to act. It is this linking of connection to journalistic
role, and the universal values and principles that undergird that role in a
democratic society, that were present in other comments that focused primarily on universal ethical principles and values.

One such group balanced the harm the photo might inflict with the potential good that might arise from an informed and aroused public:

I try to do the greater good of the people I serve; the viewers. But I would personally have a very hard time doing it because I am very sympathetic to the people I take photo/video of and of their feelings.

The parents agreed to it and it was taken in a public place. Running the picture will do good by alerting people to the situation and putting a child's face on the problem.

I think this photo is doing the greatest amount of good for the greatest amount of people.

Highlights and illustrates the problem—may be a wake-up call to many because it is so shocking.

Another participant linked to problem indirectly to government decisions:

… it illustrated a problem that affects the public and costs us dollars.

For some, the greater good included the subjects of the photo and news story:

It may help this family and others in the long run.

… the children are young enough that a correction in the direction of their lives could be beneficial.

Not running the photo amounts to protecting their parents from the consequences of what they are doing to their children.

Still others noted that such a report often could provoke official response:

The photo is graphic evidence of children imitating their parents. In this photo, parents who are drug addicts. What an environment. Photo shows the "system" needs to take control of children at risk.

People need information of all types to make a decision. I chose to run the photo because it's got enormous potential for eliciting change.

The fact that the parents signed a release also makes me feel better about the decision.

This particular photo is an example of a powerful snapshot of an issue that shows the big picture. The decision to run should not be made lightly, but a shot like this transcends the small picture.

It shows the peril the children are in and might [bring] help for them and others in similar situations.

Some linked the potential of the photo—the greater good—with other universal ethical principles:

I just thought running the photo would be best for both society and, in the long run, the children. The truth can hurt at first, but it chases away darkness.

I made my decision in the hopes of bettering society and helping children.

UNIVERSAL PRINCIPLES COMBINE IN THINKING

Truth and responsibility also were important to those participants who framed their explanations in terms of universal principles:

The truth isn't always pretty. We are charged with showing the truth As a journalist, that should be your decision.

It is the responsibility of a journalist to hold a mirror up to society—not to contribute to society's delusions. It's not the easiest path to follow—but essential nonetheless.

It was a "truthful" illustration of a serious problem. [The] picture gives valuable impact to the story.

Our job is to report news, and illustrate the story we tell as best we can, through words and images. The photo is unsettling, yes, but very telling and very powerful.

It is our job, as journalists, to present the whole truth. Yes, it might upset and anger others—but that's our job. However, it is our responsibility to present it in [a] respectful and neutral point. This would include comments from the children AND parents.

Another participant also indicated that a decision to run the photo might not be well understood by readers:

It is our job as journalists to tell the story. With the permission of the parents of a minor the story was told. If we succumb to societal pressures, then we no longer serve a purpose to our community.

Some participants indicated that they knew publishing the photograph could have a negative effect on their employers:

A compelling photo has the power to illuminate issues often denied by those who don't live in that world. This happens. If showing it can bring about positive change or educate, then it is worth publishing.

Public opinion and advertiser backlash, in other words, "what will they think" is less important. Advertisers don't dictate editorial content.

Media is are powerful medium [sic]. Running this picture could destroy all parties involved—including the newspaper.

For journalists who "saw" the issue this way, duty to community was a powerful factor in the decision:

A photograph like this tells the story without one word being written. As a journalist, I would be lax in my duty to the community in general and these kids in particular by not publishing it.

The photo showed the true story—what life for these kids is like. It was taken in a public place and the parents didn't say anything while or before it was taken. I feel it's our duty to show reality.

It is the absolute duty of a newspaper to report to its readers what is going on in the community.

To some respondents, community was not always an amorphous group of readers:

I think the public/lawmakers need to see what happens to the non-using family members who are subjected to daily interaction with those who use drugs on a regular basis. People are not always unaffected by "victimless" crimes.

Others thought of community in a very personal way:

Too often, people watch abuse or neglect or the disintegration of society before their very eyes, and they do nothing. I've been there, done that myself a few times. But that does nothing but leave the situation or person or society to waste away. As reporters, we have an obligation to show people who are living increasingly cocooned lives, to see these travails. Maybe someone will do something about them.

It is noteworthy that the journalists' decision was not monolithic. Although a majority of the participants favored running the photograph, a minority chose not to run it. However, moral development theory does not focus on outcome as much as on the process of getting there, although a reliance on universal ethical principles will, over time, lead to more systematic decision making. But, regardless of the final decision, thinking about the questions tended to reflect an appropriate use of universal ethical principles, particularly those that are a part of the utilitarian tradition and those that arise out of the duty-based approach, as reflected in the work of Immanuel Kant or W. D. Ross.

Additionally, as might be expected, these journalists were sometimes more comfortable with the words-based approach, which allowed for some expression of subtlety and nuance, than they were with the forced choices of the DIT:

> There are a number of factors that are not included that are relevant. I would need to know more about the context in which it would run. If the photo were to be presented in a way that is as simplistic and offensive as some of the sentiments expressed in the 12 questions following the descriptive passage, I would argue strongly against running it.

As the foregoing comments indicate, journalistic reasoning about this issue was both sophisticated and complex. Whether moral development schemas such as Kohlberg's, which emphasize justice, or views such as Gilligan's which emphasize connection, should predominate in moral decision making, it is clear that the professionals who took the DIT were capable of reasoning on multiple dimensions. Universal principles and universal human need for connection dominated the responses. Other elements—such as the legal ramifications, concerns about privacy, and some notions about craft—also emerged. Taken in their totality, the statements reinforced the findings of the statistical portion of the tests. These participant journalists were both able and subtle moral thinkers, a finding that should cheer the profession as well as provide an impetus for further exploration. If journalists can do this well as a profession, why is it that they still appear able to make so many boneheaded mistakes? It is to exploration of that question that this volume now turns.

Part II

THE STRUGGLE TO THINK DEEPLY—
PICTURES, DECEPTION, AND PERSUASION

CHAPTER 5

What's a Picture Worth When It Comes to Ethical Reasoning?

The world that journalists inhabit is becoming more visual and less word driven. In the 21st century, few take time to read books, newspapers, or even copy-heavy advertising. Journalists and others who produce media content hence are developing ways to communicate with fewer and fewer words. That kind of content usually features more visuals—pictures, charts, graphics, videos.

There is another, more subtle basis for this shift. Scientific research has shown that people do get a lot of information from messages communicated with visuals. It's an old saw, but a true one, that "a picture is worth a thousand words."

That photographs have special powers is another ubiquitous idea. Among other things, photographs have been credited with "altering people's minds and rearranging their lives" (Goldberg, 1991, p. 7), and bringing both "help and harm to others" (Lester, 2000, p. 57). Some even credit photographs with helping promote morality; photographs can create "moral outrage" (Sontag, 1977, p. 19) and "rouse consciences" (Goldberg, 1991, p. 199) that can lead to social reform and cultural change. There is even some anecdotal evidence to support this view. When Jacob Riis published his photographs of people living in filthy tenements, it helped lead to both efforts to clean up the slums and legislation to prevent unsanitary living conditions. Lewis Hines' photographs of children toiling in sweatshops were followed by child labor legislation. The Farm Security Administration photographers' work in the Great Depression helped promote the creation of Social Security and other welfare reforms. Television video of atrocities in Vietnam helped Americans think critically about that war. Examples abound of visual information having an effect on people's emotions and consciences.

Journalists are well aware of the power of photographs; some news organizations even have policies prohibiting photos of dead bodies or pictures that show blood. When newspapers and TV news do run such pictures, journalists tell how calls from irate subscribers pour in. One former managing editor of a major daily newspaper says that whenever running such a photograph is contemplated, "It raises the level of ethical discussion. Journalists make better arguments when there is a picture" (J. Bolch personal communication with former managing editor of the Raleigh, NC-based *News and Observer*).

PICTURES ARE POWERFUL FOR MULTIPLE REASONS

This chapter explores the connection between visual images and ethical reasoning. The impetus for the studies described here was a preliminary finding from the pilot study of 72 journalists who took the DIT; the dilemma that was accompanied by a photograph garnered the highest ethical reasoning score (mean ethics score = 19.1, $SD = 18.9$), a score that was significantly higher, in a statistical sense, than were the reasoning scores for four other dilemmas ($t = 14.05$, $df = 71$, $p < .001$). That result was tantalizing, even though it is well known that a survey such as the DIT can't determine causality. However, the question lingered: Did photos influence journalists' ethical reasoning?

As indicated in chapter 1, moral development as detailed by Piaget emerged from a game with a visual component—marbles. Research into the workings of the brain has provided evidence that there may, in fact, be a biological reason for the difference in ethical reasoning when visual information is included. Scientists who study the anatomy of the brain have long known that speech and writing are physically processed on one side of the brain (the left), whereas emotions and images are processed on the other (Levin & Divine-Hawkins, 1974). This split-brain theory has been confirmed with brain imaging data showing that thinking in images is different from thinking in language, and that the two types of thinking result in different outcomes (Paivio, 1986). When left-hemisphere data such as written or spoken words enter a person's brain, they follow a certain route through specific structures. These structures process the information logically and analytically—it's all somewhat consciously controlled. In contrast, when a person sees a scene or a picture, or experiences an emotion, that information takes a very different route through the brain, encountering different processing structures. This route—through the right side of the brain—is automatic, immediate, and unthinking (Barry, 1997; Paivio, 1983).

Despite these different routes through the cerebral cortex, visual information isn't necessarily inferior to verbal information. Processing visual information with this different route—the same route, incidentally, that emotions travel—allows the brain to attach emotional significance to information. Positive emotions have been shown to significantly increase P scores on the DIT (Olejnik & LaRue, 1980). Emotions, of course, aren't always positive. Other studies have shown that empathy affects moral behavior, and empathy is strongly connected to emotion (Hoffman, 2000). In fact, empathy is defined as feeling what another person feels, positive or negative.

Besides this biological evidence, there are some well-accepted theories that explain how people think and reason—psychologists call it "cognitive processing"—that point to the photograph as contributing to this higher level of thinking about ethical issues. Several theories acknowledge the biological evidence of two sides of the brain with two different functions, and build on that knowledge to propose that not only are visual and verbal information cognitively different, but they also can be connected and pooled. This pooled information can be superior to information from only one mode (Paivio, 1983). Numerous studies have shown that these theories are correct when it comes to memory; information presented both visually and verbally is better remembered. That's one reason why children's books have so many pictures (Levin & Mayer, 1993; Madigan, 1983). Theory and research suggest this redundant information—repeating the same thing in the different forms of pictures and words—increases the likelihood that it will be processed through at least one route if not two, and that it will be better remembered. Advertisers routinely employ this approach.

However, enhanced memory isn't the only reason that adding pictures to ethical problems might improve a person's quality of thought. Getting information in two forms is expected to lead to thinking about the issue more deeply. Pictures—at least ones that show something unusual or novel—have been shown to encourage what scientists call "mental elaboration," or thinking about something. Mental elaboration, which is based in research findings about the two ways the brain processes information, suggests that people process messages in the two ways that mirror the brain's physical structures. One way, called the *central route*, requires thinking before forming an attitude. The second, called the *peripheral route*, doesn't require as much thought, similar to the right-brain route taken by pictures and emotions. Visual information can be processed by either route, with the key being whether a person has the ability or motivation to make the effort required to process it by the central, deep-thinking route (Petty &

Cacioppo, 1986). Ordinary, unexciting pictures probably travel the peripheral or unthinking route, but novel or shocking pictures—ones that attract attention and hold it—encourage central route processing. It is this type of processing—the kind involving serious thought—that these studies investigated. The photographs used here were chosen specifically because they had the qualities that have been shown to cause viewers to think.

Thus, a central premise of this research is that novel, attention-getting photographs that illustrate these ethical dilemmas will increase people's attention to or involvement with the dilemmas. Increased attention and involvement will result in more—and better—ethical reasoning.

In addition to theories describing how the brain works, research on the effects of photographs also supports this line of inquiry. Photographs have been shown to have powerful effects on people's memory, attention, emotions, involvement, and perceptions (Brosius, 1993; Garcia & Stark, 1991; Husselbee & Adams, 1996). Stories with photographs are more likely to be read than are stories without such visuals, and the bigger the photo the better (Huh, 1994). Readers learn more and remember information from stories better if they have a photograph than if they don't. This is especially true when the photos are vivid or arouse curiosity (Gibson & Zillmann, 2000). Photographs alone have even been shown to alter people's perceptions of what stories are important, something researchers call an *agenda-setting* effect (Wanta, 1988).

THE EFFECT OF PICTURES AND EMOTION

Besides conveying information, pictures also affect people's emotions. They make the information more touching than words alone can muster (Burgoon, 1980; Meyrowitz, 1985; Pryluck, 1976). As well, pictures can alter people's perceptions and influence their judgment (Gibson, Zillmann, & Sargent, 1999; Grimes & Drechsel, 1996) even when the information in the photos is not mentioned in the text (Gibson & Zillmann, 2000). Given these findings, it's not far off to suggest that pictures can influence ethical thinking.

The studies reported in this chapter looked at the effects of pictures on other kinds of cognitive processes such as memory, attention, involvement, and perceptions, and examined whether the power of photos translated into different thinking about ethical issues. Novel or unexpected photos should increase attention and involvement with the dilemmas they illustrate. That attention and involvement should translate into more rigorous thinking. Because information is both visual and verbal, the dilemmas with photographs should be processed using the central route. In sum, photographs will convey information about the social problems and the people involved in them that is qualitatively different, and that difference should, in turn, result in higher-level ethical reasoning.

This is important, because if photographs do improve ethical reasoning, then adding photos to the mix when people consider ethical issues may improve the outcomes. This book is concerned with the ethical reasoning of journalists, so these studies were conducted on journalism students. However, the lessons learned may apply to people in all professions.

PHOTOS, EXPERIMENTS, AND THEIR RESULTS

The way these studies were conducted was explained in detail in chapter 2. To summarize, the DIT was adapted to be suitable for experiments. Four new dilemmas were written that focused on typical journalistic problems. Experiments identify cause and effect by strictly controlling the conditions in the study; the four dilemmas were all the same word length, and all asked the same questions in exactly the same order. All scenarios were set in a newspaper of an unspecified size to control for possible perceived differences in ethical standards between print and broadcast and between large and small newspapers. Half the participants read the ethical dilemmas *and* saw photographs that went with them; the other half read identical dilemmas but did not see photos. This allowed us to determine if the photographs had an influence on ethical reasoning. As it turns out, it is not an infrequent occurrence in newsrooms that journalists involved in making ethical decisions about photographs may not see the photographs. Furthermore, it is more frequent that those people making newsroom decisions never see or interact with the people affected by those decisions. For example, managing editors and others in the upper levels of the news organization do not routinely see or talk to the people in stories, yet these high-level journalists may have the final say.

The photographs were used with permission of the Pictures of the Year organization, or POY. This is a prestigious national competition among newspapers and magazines, and the winning photographs become the property of the University of Missouri School of Journalism, the competition's sponsor. All photographs used in this study had been published. The dilemmas in most cases were fashioned after real stories that ran with the photographs.

The scenarios used in the experiments were as follows:

- In one dilemma, a photojournalist is working on a story about children who imitate their parents' drug use, and shoots a compelling photograph of a 5-year-old girl with rubber tubing wrapped around her arm and a syringe pointed at her forearm, pretending to inject IV drugs. The real photograph was taken by Bradley Clift, a staff photographer at the *Hartford* (CT) *Courant* at the time, and won an award in the 1999 POY contest. The dilemma written for these studies explained that the photograph was taken in a public place and the children's parents have given the photographer permission to take pictures. Afterward, the children's grandmother called the photographer and asked that the paper not run the photograph. (For complete wording of dilemmas, see the Appendix.) This is the same story and photograph that was included in the DIT survey reported in this book. This scenario is patterned after an actual case (Borden, 1996).

- In the second scenario, a journalist is investigating complaints of abuse and neglect of elderly patients by home health care providers. Investigations by authorities have been stymied by a lack of evidence and by elderly witnesses who may be unconvincing in court. Authorities encourage the journalist to pursue the story. For the participants who see photos, this picture shows an elderly man who has become emaciated after being neglected by his home health providers. This photo was taken by Brian Plonka and won the 1998 POY contest. In the dilemma, the elderly man sees the picture and gives permission for the newspaper to run it. However, his adult children hear about it and call to ask that it not be used. This is the same story used in the DIT survey study, except that no picture was provided in the survey and the decision that survey participants had to make was whether to run the story using anonymous sources.

- The third dilemma focused on a teenage prostitute. The journalist is reporting about young girls who get pregnant, are abandoned by family and boyfriends, and are unable to negotiate the welfare system. In order to survive, they turn to prostitution, which often occurs in the one-room apartments they share with their small children. The photographer who took this picture is Eugene Richards, widely acknowledged as one of the greatest photographers today. He was working for Magnum at the time he made this photograph, which won a Pictures of the Year award and went on to be included in a book of his photographs, *Cocaine True, Cocaine Blue* (Richards, 1994). In the story for these experiments, the social worker assigned to the young prostitute's case requests that the picture not be used.

- The final scenario is about domestic violence. A journalist is working on a story about a recent increase in women, married to middle- and upper-class businessmen, who have been showing up in emergency rooms with signs of physical abuse. The picture was taken by Meri Simon, a staff photographer with the San Jose (CA) *Mercury News* at the time; it was a 1999 POY winner. In the experimental dilemma, the photographer had permission from the hospital to take pictures, and the woman in the picture not only signed the release but encouraged the photographer to publish it, saying that if this could happen to her it could happen to anyone and she wanted people to be aware. However, the woman's sister calls to ask that the newspaper not run the photo after the woman refused to press charges against her husband.

For the second experiment in this series, the domestic violence story and picture were replaced with a story and photo about homeless children. This was done so that the study would have two dilemmas about children and two about adults, and that people who saw photos would see two photos of white people and two photos of African-American people. These alterations help to provide assurance that any effects on ethical reasoning were caused by the photographs and not something else, such as age or race of the people in the photographs.

- The homeless story centered on a family who lives in cheap, dirty motels on good days and in their van on bad ones. The photographer has a picture of a child, crouched on a dirty floor, tipping a cereal bowl into her mouth to drain the last drop of milk. The child's teacher asks that the photograph not run. This photograph was also a POY contest winner, taken by Chris Tyree when he was a student at Ohio State University.

The participants in these experiments were 194 journalism students in the first study, and 103 in the second run.

The idea that visual information has the power to affect ethical reasoning was borne out by these studies. Both discerned that photographs did have the ability to change participants' ethical reasoning for the better. In the second study, photographs alone were enough to elevate all participants' ethical reasoning. This overall finding is significant, and there are other findings of note.

In the first study, photographs made a positive difference only for participants who weren't very involved with the ethical dilemma. "Uninvolved" participants were defined as those who said they felt the dilemmas weren't particularly important, didn't feel very involved or concerned about them, and didn't care much about the people in them (Cronbach's $\alpha = .93$). Showing photographs to these uninvolved participants somehow helped their ethical reasoning climb to new heights. The ethical reasoning scores of those who saw photographs ($M = 20.4$, $SD = 4.8$) were significantly better than were those of low-involved participants who didn't see photographs ($M = 16.4$, $SD = 5.2$; $F = 5.57$, $df = 1,193$, $p < .01$).

In the second study, average ethical reasoning scores were higher for all those who saw photographs ($M = 21.08$, $SD = 4.72$), regardless of how involved they were, when compared to participants who didn't see photographs ($M = 17.02$, $SD = 6.36$; $F = 13.61$, $df = 1,102$, $p < .001$).

In the first study, the effect of photographs was most likely masked by other things; for example, the first study also asked people to write down all the thoughts they had about each dilemma. It took people in the first study more than twice as long to complete the questionnaire than it did people in the second study. It's possible they just got tired and couldn't concentrate, something known as "fatigue" in research.

When the study was shortened for the second go-round, the effect of photographs only previously hinted at emerged clearly—photographs by themselves did indeed improve ethical reasoning. This effect has been reproduced in yet another study; that study is reported in chapter 6. Although the third study was designed to explore other influences on ethical reasoning, it was still conducted by the method outlined previously: Half the participants saw the photographs and half did not. Seeing photos resulted in significantly higher levels of ethical reasoning ($M = 18.56$, $SD = 6.0$) than did not seeing photos ($M = 15.6$, $SD = 5.6$; $F = 5.6$, $df = 1,107$, $p < .05$).

It is well documented that adding pictures to a story leads to better learning and memory (Graber, 1990; Madigan, 1983), especially when the pictures are vivid or arouse curiosity (Gibson & Zillman, 2000). In light of these findings, it should not be so surprising that adding pictures to an ethical dilemma also leads to better reasoning about ethical information. Compelling images have been shown to change the way people process information (Newhagen & Reeves, 1992). Based on these results, we suggest that those changes in processing apply to the processing of ethical information.

PICTURES AND STAKEHOLDERS: MORAL WEIGHT FOR THE SUBJECTS OF NEWS ACCOUNTS

Both studies also consistently found one thing that was an important element in ethical reasoning: the ability and willingness to consider the effect of publication on those who would be affected by news stories—the stakeholders. Stakeholders included those who were pictured as well as other people and institutions involved.

Seeing photographs made people think about stakeholders more (Study 1: photo mean = 15.4, SD = 3.1, no photo mean = 14.7, SD = 3.2, F = 4.3, df = 1,193, p < .05; Study 2: photo mean = 14.02, SD = 3.15, no photo mean = 12.69, SD = 3; F = 4.8, df = 1,102, p < .05). Also, more thoughts about stakeholders produced better ethical reasoning (Study 1: F = 3.8, df = 1,190, p < .05; Study 2: F = 4.07, df = 1,102, p < .05).

Although statistical analysis supported this view, the participants' comments about their thought process, detailed in chapter 4, provided additional evidence that seeing photos promoted this change in thought patterns. Readers will recall those responses were attached to a survey, however, the statistical findings are consistent. As theory predicted, using both visual and verbal systems in the brain may be partly responsible for this. The use of two systems in the brain may lead to greater elaboration, or more thinking about a topic, which then results in higher-quality ethical reasoning.

However, this improvement in ethical reasoning was not consistent for all sorts of thoughts, although the addition of visual information did encourage thinking about a variety of topics. The experiments also measured how much people thought about the journalists in the dilemmas and the newspaper's readers. Participants also indicated whether their thoughts were positive, negative, or neutral. Thinking about the journalists themselves or about newspaper readers did not produce the same improvement in ethical reasoning as did thinking about stakeholders, nor did it matter whether the thoughts were positive, negative, or neutral.

It's intuitive that thinking about stakeholders is especially influential in ethical reasoning; the consequences of an ethical decision are felt most by the people who have the greatest to lose or gain. Others do have a stake in the outcomes. Journalists spend time and effort making pictures, and reporting and writing stories; audiences might be upset at the breakfast table upon seeing such photographs. However, the journalists' and audiences' stakes are not as great as are those of the people who are the focus of news.

From another perspective, photographs may tend to direct attention to the people whose images appear in the photographs rather than toward journalists or audiences. The importance to ethical reasoning of thinking about stakeholders is intriguing because thinking only about one group of people is not a hallmark of higher ethical reasoning; the idea of universal principles demands that all of society be considered equally.

EMOTIONAL RESPONSE DOESN'T
NECESSARILY BOOST ETHICAL THINKING

Something else that played an important role in improving ethical reasoning was how involved the participants felt with the stories. As noted earlier, when people thought the dilemmas were not particularly important, engaging, or interesting, having photographs to look at caused their ethical reasoning to improve. Those low-involved people were significantly more likely to make better ethical decisions when they saw photographs than when they did not.

This finding that people who were not very involved but thought at a higher level when they saw photographs dovetails with the results of other studies. Psychologists have found that people who are not very involved in the outcome of a situation are most likely to respond to superficial or peripheral cues (Petty, Cacioppo, & Goldman, 1981). In the experiments presented in this chapter, photographs served as powerful peripheral cues under conditions of low involvement. Just as the psychologists found that effects are strongest for the uninvolved—those who are most likely to respond to superficial cues as a convenient shortcut—participants in this study who were uninvolved responded in the same pattern.

It is not surprising that photographs had the ability to induce significant changes in ethical reasoning for this group. When people are interested in a topic, think it is important, and feel involved, they are more likely to pay attention to information about the topic and think about it more deeply. However, people are often confronted with topics that are not personally relevant, useful, or interesting. Rather than exerting a great deal of cognitive effort to evaluate the situation, people use less effort and concentrate on peripheral cues such as photographs.

The effect of photographs on the casual viewer would seem to be a plausible explanation for what happened to the participants in this study. Those who were not personally invested in the ethical dilemmas did not expend a great deal of cognitive effort, and less effort resulted in lower levels of ethical reasoning. However, when uninterested people saw photographs, it bumped up their ethical reasoning. For people who were highly involved, they were already engaged in thorough processing of the problem, scrutinizing the different points of view and evaluating the arguments. Under this condition, a peripheral cue such as a photograph was simply a drop in the information bucket that made no significant ripples in these participants' ethical reasoning.

In a laboratory study, the artificiality of the conditions may reasonably be expected to lead to low involvement in participants. But it is not hard to imagine when working journalists might operate under conditions of low involvement—those facing deadlines that limit the time they have to process the arguments thoroughly, for example. Television journalists especially may experience this. Instead of processing information thoroughly, journalists under pressure may rely on visuals as a convenient shortcut. Under these conditions, this study shows that visuals can be a valuable addition to ethical decision making: They boost the quality of ethical reasoning when conditions are not conducive to high involvement. Mere exposure to visual stimuli operates most clearly when people are essentially unthinking.

There is even the possibility that low involvement can result because journalists simply fail to recognize that there is an ethical issue to be dealt with. The first step in Rest's Four-Component Model of ethical reasoning (Rest, 1983) is what he called "moral sensitivity," or simply interpreting the situation as involving an ethical issue: "Imagine a person who fails to act morally because it just didn't occur to him or her that something he or she might be doing [or could do] would affect other people" (Rest & Narvaez, 1984, p. 23). This failure of the ethical imagination has been the case in numerous real-life dilemmas; for example, when *Time* magazine editors darkened O. J. Simpson's photograph. At the time that decision was made, the only considerations were aesthetic. It was only later, when a barrage of criticism erupted, that the journalists recognized the ethical implications (as well as the racial ones) of what they had done. The evidence from *Time's* editors and the O. J. Simpson photograph is supported by more systematic scholarly work. A study that explored the thought processes of journalists who were sued for invasion of privacy found that these journalists "did not seem particularly adept at recognizing" a potential legal problem (Voakes, 1998, p. 388). Of the 42 journalists interviewed, only 19 remembered being especially aware of legal issues. This is not particularly unique to journalists, Voakes noted; many defendants in all domains are surprised when they are sued. This kind of ethical unawareness could be an example of a situation that would produce low involvement in journalists faced with ethical decisions; it is then that the addition of visual images may prove beneficial.

The lesson that journalists can take from this is that rather than discussing ethical issues without benefit of visual images, they should become aware of the effect of visuals on their ethical decisions. They can ask if there are photographs of the people in the story around whom the ethical question revolves. Mid- and top-level editors can be made aware that their decisions may be improved by considering all the evidence—including the visual evidence. Furthermore, consciously choosing to include visual evidence in decision-making routines is simple and inexpensive, and imminently easier to manipulate than are some of the other variables that have been found to affect ethical reasoning, such as age, education, newsroom socialization, and organization ownership. Incorporating visual evidence into routine, decision-making processes requires little more than awareness, a few requests, and a small investment of time. Yet, it may be one giant step toward improving the quality of journalists' ethical reasoning that also may help improve the outcome that audiences see and critique.

Although these studies didn't examine empathy as feeling what another person feels, they did ask about the emotions people felt while reading the stories. The power of emotion that has long been attributed to photographs was confirmed in these studies; photographs alone do have the ability to make people feel emotions more intensely. When people saw pictures of those involved in an ethical dilemma, not only did the photographs make them think about those people more, but they also made the respondents worry more and feel sadder, more disgusted, and angry (photo mean = 7.62, SD = 2.26; no photo mean = 7.22, SD = 2.23, F = 3.5, df = 1,193, p < .05). However, this connection between photos and emotions did not extend to ethical reasoning. In other words, emotion by itself was not enough to prod participants to think more deeply about ethical issues. Seeing photographs was significantly related to greater emotional intensity, but not to different levels of ethical reasoning. This finding makes sense considering that previous studies on emotion and ethical reasoning found that only positive emotions elevated ethical reasoning, not negative emotions like the ones engendered by these photos (Olejnik & LaRue, 1980).

Despite sharing common physiological processing (emotions and visuals are both processed in the right hemisphere of the brain), greater emotional intensity did not affect ethical reasoning the way that photographs did. The same theory that helped explain the impact of photographs on those who were less involved with the scenarios helps to explain this finding as well. If people process pictures deeply and with much cognitive effort, then the photos are actually acting as central cues that have the ability to affect attitudes and behavior in a lasting way. Novel photographs like these should be processed more deeply than should typical ones. Emotions are rarely processed so deeply and cognitively. Theory suggests that peripheral cues do not override central route processing. Thus, the peripheral cue of an emotion-laden photograph would not be expected to change the quality of ethical reasoning.

THE THEORETICAL IMPLICATIONS: PICTURES CAN AID ETHICAL THINKING

This study concerned itself with the ethical reasoning of journalists. Never have the media been so criticized for their ethical behavior; factors that can be used to improve journalists' ethical reasoning, and thus behavior, are of the utmost importance. However, beyond the ethical reasoning quality of journalists is the media's ability to affect the thinking and reasoning of the audience. If, as Barry asserted, "Images are a means of communication that runs deeper and is ultimately more powerful than words in its ability to condition attitudes and to form thoughts" (Barry, 1997, p. 338), then the profession should bring its more powerful weapons to bear on this problem.

Finally, the findings of this study make an important theoretical contribution to the scholarship of moral development. Pictures matter; they can influence the quality of ethical reasoning. As scholars in other disciplines continue to investigate moral development, they should ask their study participants not only what they were thinking, but also what they were seeing.

CHAPTER 6

Ethical Reasoning
and the Color Bind

Race has been acknowledged as being at the root of one of America's greatest problems. Despite recent decades of intense focus geared toward changing the way people are treated because of their skin color, America still struggles with issues of racial profiling, discrimination in hiring and promotion practices, and unequal access to housing, education, and almost everything else basic to human life. To be sure, things have improved from the days when African Americans couldn't eat in restaurants or had to drive roundtrip to events because they were allowed in hotels only to clean or carry bags. However, racial prejudice remains an enduring problem.

Also enduring is the criticism that the media contribute to this problem because of the way they portray ethnic and racial groups, especially African Americans (Entman, 1990, 1992, 1994; Poindexter & Stroman, 1981). Television shows that characterize blacks as shuffling Amos 'n' Andy types or newspaper photos that show a disproportionate number of criminals who are African American contribute to readers and viewers forming negative attitudes and stereotypes (Chiricos, Eschholz, & Gertz, 1997; Gilliam & Iyengar, 2000; Valentino, 1999). Yet, such portrayals continue despite journalists' efforts to eliminate racial prejudice from news accounts. Most newsrooms prohibit the routine reporting of race unless it is a necessary part of the story—to capture a criminal on the loose, for example. However, racial bias and stereotypical portrayals still manage to creep into the news in more subtle ways.

The journalism industry and its scholars have spent tremendous time and effort examining how and why these stereotypes persist. There is much research that explores the roots of the decisions journalists make that result in racially biased news. The study reported in this chapter again looks at journalists' ethical reasoning, but this time through the lens of color. The

82

twist here is that this study is not concerned with the race of the *journalist*, like most studies of this type, but instead with the race of the *people* about whom the journalist is making decisions. Journalists, like the audiences they influence, also may have negative perceptions about people from certain racial groups. It seems logical that those perceptions might make a difference in journalists' news judgment despite their best efforts to avoid prejudicial thinking. The study reported in this chapter puts that logic to an experimental test.

THE ORIGINS OF STEREOTYPES

The word *stereotype* has a bad reputation; it's almost always viewed as a negative thing, even though it didn't start out that way. Originally, the idea of a stereotype didn't necessarily even apply to race. A stereotype was basically a script that described the typical person, event, or object of a certain category (Abbott, Black, & Smith, 1985). For example, a typical doctor wears a white coat, not a blue jumpsuit. A typical meal at a restaurant starts with ordering, then eating, then paying, not the reverse. A typical car is not a double-decker bus. People form stereotypes from their past experiences; having seen the same thing repeatedly, they learn to expect events to unfold in a certain order, scenes to look a certain way, and certain types of people to look and behave in a certain manner (Mandler, 1984). Originally, these stereotypes—another word common in academic circles is *schemas*—were considered to be good things. These mental representations of the way things usually are help people cope with what would otherwise be a flood of new information (Graber, 1988). If you had no schema for a doctor, for example, you'd be shocked when one asked you to take off your clothes! Instead, stereotypes help make everyday interactions easier. They help people process information efficiently rather than become overwhelmed by it (Cohen, 1981). But just as most good things can be taken too far, so can stereotypes. When the views people develop about certain races of people become too general and negative, they can lead to inappropriate stereotyping and prejudice that is often reflected in actual behavior.

Philosophers have another way of articulating this problem. Stereotypes lead people to judge others—or the acts of others—based on the category of the actor, *not* the actions of an individual. Treating individual people based on some general category that could represent them—all short people, all tall people, all women, all men, and so on—not only represents sloppy thinking, it is at its core unjust. Yet, philosophy, too, does accept that membership in certain sorts of categories—for example, children or other vulnerable actors—can be a logical and justifiable reason for treating all people who fit in a certain category in a particular way. This thinking is even the root of some laws; the criminal justice system treats children differently than it does adults precisely because children fit the general category of "child."

Whether your thinking about stereotypes has more in common with philosophy or psychology, the same problem surfaces in both disciplines. Appropriately used, stereotypes can be helpful, with daily living as well as with ethical decision making. Inappropriate or unthinking use of stereotypes, however, can create real problems, particularly when such thinking surfaces in the workplace and influences how professionals do their jobs.

STEREOTYPING HAPPENS AUTOMATICALLY

There are stereotypes about almost everything, not just race; gender is another good example (Grimes & Drechsel, 1996). People expect men to behave differently from women and to hold different roles. A behavior or trait that is seen as positive in a man may be interpreted as negative in a woman, or vice versa. Women politicians may get emotional without it hurting their careers, but a man who shows the same feelings in public may never hold office again. Just as there are schemas for race, gender, occupations, and experiences such as eating at restaurants, psychologists have also theorized that there are schemas for different types of thinking; ethical decision making is one of them (Rest et al., 1999). People have schemas, or typical ideas, about ethical problems that they have learned from past experience. They use these ethical schemas when making decisions about new ethical problems.

Researchers in this field of moral development believe that people develop their ethical reasoning abilities as children by starting at the lowest quality stages and rising through the ranks (Kohlberg, 1981, 1984). As noted in chapter 1, not everyone reaches the highest level; most people operate in the middle range. However, if people have learned to operate at the highest stage, they are capable of applying that good-quality reasoning to ethical situations, although they may not always do so. It turns out that most people operate most of the time in the middle range, but they are also capable of rising to higher levels at some times and sinking to lower levels at others. It is this ebb and flow of ethical reasoning quality that may be taking place when people with negative stereotypes about certain races of people make ethical decisions about those people. It's not that they are necessarily ethically challenged, but instead that something from their schemas about race causes them to regress and use lower-quality ethical reasoning when making decisions involving people of that race.

American society has acknowledged that prejudice against minorities is undesirable and there are efforts to eliminate discrimination against them. Yet, progress has been slow. There may be more to the reasons for this than a mere unwillingness to change. Psychologists working to understand racial bias have come to the conclusion that stereotyping occurs automatically for most people, and is difficult if not impossible to control. Studies have shown that even people who don't intend to be biased are in fact biased (Stocking & Gross, 1989), and this applies to racial biases too. Negative stereotypes about African Americans are subtle and persistent, even in people who claim not to be prejudiced (Devine, 1989; Gaertner & McLaughlin, 1983). These stereotypes are evoked in people automatically, without them even being aware that it is happening (Devine & Monteith, 1999). Although some studies have discovered techniques that people can use to keep from reacting automatically to such stereotypes (Devine & Monteith, 1999), other researchers have found that stereotypes creep in anyway (Bargh, 1999).

This automatic and unconscious use of stereotypes may be what is occurring in journalists who produce news content that conveys a subtle yet still racist message. When journalists have to make choices that are ethically ambiguous, this automatic, unconscious activation of stereotypes can have devastating consequences when race is also a factor. Their decisions, if not based on good-quality ethical reasons, can hurt not only the individuals involved but also the entire journalism profession and the goal of social equality.

RACE IN OTHER KINDS OF REASONING

Although there appears to be no research directly investigating the effect of race on journalists' ethical reasoning, many have examined the relationship between race and other kinds of cognitive processes. For example, people tend to remember things that are consistent with their stereotypes of blacks as criminals and whites as victims (Grimes & Drechsel, 1996; Levy, 2000; Oliver & Fonash, 2002). Even when stories identify a black victim and a white perpetrator, people will "misremember" it the other way around, the way that is consistent with their schemas.

In one study that was not about journalists, the race of the people in the stories had an effect on the reasoning of those who had to make ethical decisions that would affect the people in the stories. This study used the same instrument as the study reported here to gauge ethical reasoning, and in that study, when the stories were exactly the same and only the race of the people in them changed, blacks suffered (Locke & Tucker, 1988). Using as a base the findings of this one study on race and ethical reasoning and many other studies on race and other kinds of reasoning, the research reported in this chapter looks at how racial stereotypes affect ethical reasoning of journalistic dilemmas.

THE ISSUE OF SOCIAL ISSUES

As in most things, context makes a difference in ethical decisions. It is perfectly logical to expect different decisions in different situations, even if the question is the same. For example, you might choose to tell a lie at a party that you would not tell on the witness stand in court. Context does matter, and you can't have an ethical dilemma without putting it into some kind of context. The ethical dilemmas that were created for this study were set in different contexts—one is about drugs, one about prostitution, one about homelessness, and another about elder abuse. Ethical reasoning about criminal behavior, such as drug use, might understandably evoke different thoughts and emotions than might issues such as homelessness, which is terrible but not illegal. Hence, it is understandable to assume that people might come to different decisions in different circumstances, even when the problem is the same. In this experiment, participants were asked to answer the same question: Should a particular photograph be published? But because the story contexts were different, it is reasonable that different decisions might result. For example, one person might choose to run the picture of the elderly man who was abused but not run the photo of the child pretending to use drugs, because that person believes children should be protected more than adults should. Someone else might argue that because drug use is such a serious problem, publicity about it will do more good for society, and thus that photo should be used. So, for this study, it was expected that whatever issue the story was about (the context) would make a difference in ethical reasoning.

It was also possible that different social issues carried subtle connotations of race. This is what scholars call "racial coding"—when an issue becomes tacitly identified with a specific racial minority, people automatically think of people of that race even though it may never be mentioned explicitly. For example, when the subject of welfare comes up, it is not uncommon for people to automatically associate it with African Americans. Immigration may be similarly be associated with Hispanics. Even different types of drugs and crime have come to be racially coded—crack cocaine, for example, is said to be associated with blacks, whereas powder cocaine is purportedly associated with whites (Reeves & Campbell, 1994). As one scholar put it, "Quite clearly, 'black crime' does not make people think about tax evasion or embezzling from brokerage firms. Rather, the offenses generally associated with blacks are those ... involving violence ..." (Hacker, 1995, p. 188). By using four stories set in the context of four different social issues, the study reported here examined whether the social issue the dilemma is about also drives ethical reasoning, and whether it is intertwined with the race of the people in the stories.

THE STUDY'S DESIGN

This study asked participants to read the same four journalism-related ethical dilemmas that were used in the study that looked at photographs (reported in the preceding chapter). To briefly recap, they involved an elderly man left emaciated by his home health care workers, two children who imitated their drug-addicted parents by playing a game of "junkie," a prostitute, and a homeless family. For all four dilemmas, participants decided whether to run a photograph or not after somebody associated with the people in the photos had requested that the photographs not be used. Half the participants received stories with photographs, and half did not.

The photographs were key to this study because the visuals were the mechanism by which information about race was conveyed. By not explicitly telling participants that race was an issue when introducing the experiment, or not pointing out the race of people in the story text, it was expected that the racial information would be processed the way this type of information is naturally processed. It was important that the study not draw attention to the issue of race so that participants would answer honestly and not fall victim to what social scientists call the "social desirability bias," by which people give the answer they perceive to be "right" according to social norms, rather than the answer they would give if their actions weren't being scrutinized by others. This study focused on whether people's racial stereotypes would affect their ethical reasoning; we did not want people to realize that race was what we were interested in and then have them give answers that were not reflective of what they truly would do under normal circumstances.

This study was able to determine if race was the deciding factor in people's ethical decisions because the race of the people in the photos was the only thing that was changed. The length and text of the story was identical, regardless of the race of those shown in the photographs. The photographs themselves were digitally altered to vary the skin tone, hair, and facial features in each image. Except for skin color, hair, and facial features, the photographs of white people were identical to the photographs of black people. So, for example, there was a photograph of an elderly black man and a photograph of an elderly white man; a photograph of a homeless black child and a photograph of a homeless white child, and so on. Each participant in the study got two stories with photographs of blacks and two stories with photographs of whites. The story order and the race of the people in the photographs that accompanied them were rotated at random. Hence, for example, one participant might see black people for the homeless and drug stories and white people for the prostitution and elder abuse stories, whereas another participant saw the exact opposite—white people in the homeless and drug stories and black people in the prostitution and elder abuse stories. There were 16 variations of story and race.

The stories were written to be as racially ambiguous as possible; for example, the fictitious names of the story subjects were written to be ethnically neutral, so that people who didn't see any photographs would be less likely to associate a particular race with the people in a story. As in the previous study of photographs, winners of the prestigious Pictures of the Year awards were used so that the people making the decisions whether to run the photographs would not base their decisions on the quality of the photos.

THE RESULTS: RACE MATTERS

The same type of questionnaire was used in this study as in the photographs study. The goal of the questionnaire was to see whether people's level of ethical reasoning changed when the only thing that was different was whether the people in the dilemmas were black or white.[1]

For this study, which was also given to college students majoring in journalism and mass communication, approximately half of the 108 participants saw photographs and half did not. The 53 who knew the race of the people in the dilemmas because they saw photographs demonstrated significantly lower levels of ethical reasoning when the people in the photos were black than when they were white (mean ethics score, black photos = 4.3, SD = 1.93; mean ethics score, white photos = 4.98, SD = 1.91; F = 4.73, df = 1, 52, p < .05).

---

[1]This study was confined to people representing two races, African American and Caucasian, in the interest of controlling the conditions of the experiment. Future studies should expand this inquiry to people of different races, including Asian, Hispanic, Native American, and so on.

This result shows that race does have the ability to affect people's ethical reasoning about journalistic decisions, as would be expected from what scholars know about the way stereotypes and schemas work. When the participants in this study saw an African American in the photographs, their ethical reasoning suffered. They made ethical decisions based on higher-quality reasoning when they knew the people in the dilemmas were white. Nothing else changed except the race of the people in the photographs; the length, wording, and all other aspects of the ethical dilemmas were exactly the same, regardless of the race of the people in the photos.

Race also was responsible for explaining the most about why people differed in their ethical reasoning ($\eta^2 = .083$); that is, statistical tests that measure why people's answers vary placed the reason for most of this variation on race, even more than on other explanations including the story issue ($\eta^2 = .061$) and whether a person saw a photo ($\eta^2 = .045$).

The issue that the story was about also mattered, as was expected. People used the poorest-quality ethical reasoning when the issue was prostitution (mean ethics score = 3.73, $SD = 2.5$), followed by homelessness (mean ethics score = 4.11, $SD = 2.48$), and then drugs (mean ethics score = 4.43, $SD = 2.33$). The best-quality ethical reasoning, regardless of the race of the people in the photos, was afforded to the issue of elder abuse (mean ethics score = 4.98, $SD = 2.2$). As was indicated in chapter 4 by professional journalists' written responses, this result provides some statistical support to the notion that journalists' ethical thinking can (but does not always) include a justification that permits doing "bad things to bad people."

Interestingly, however, ethical reasoning was not affected by some combination of story issue and race ($F = .107$, $df = 3$, $p = .96$). That is, people used about the same-quality ethical reasoning for the prostitution story with photos of blacks as for the story with whites, and so on. Ethical reasoning suffered when the people in the photos were black, but it did not suffer significantly more because of the story issue—prostitution versus homelessness, for example. Another way of putting it is that race had an effect on ethical reasoning, and story issue had an effect on ethical reasoning, but the combination of race and story issue together did not have an exponentially greater effect.

This study extends previous research showing that race matters in the kinds of thinking that results in memory, attitudes, and perceptions, to include the finding that race matters to ethical thinking as well. Now we know that race can affect the reasoning of people making ethical decisions, and in this experiment, African Americans are the ones who would suffer most.

Time and again, research has shown that people have harsher attitudes and worse opinions of blacks than of whites. It should come as little surprise that people, including future journalists, use poorer-quality reasons when they make ethical choices about African Americans than when they make choices about Caucasians. Stereotypical ideas about race have been shown to influence everything from whom we blame for crime and violence, to the kinds of punishment we endorse, to the very "facts" that we remember. Furthermore, these stereotypical ideas are called up automatically, even in people who claim not to be prejudiced. This kind of thinking is almost subliminal in that people lack critical awareness of the fact that they are being subconsciously affected by biases. Then, people attribute their attitudes to something other than race.

Research has indicated that subliminal perception occurs on the side of the brain responsible for visual processing. Thus, we may be particularly susceptible to prejudice when processing visual information—the kind most likely to tell us about a person's race. This would seem to be a reasonable explanation for what was going on with the participants in this study; their racial stereotypes may be automatically and unconsciously called up when they see a person's race in a photograph, and that results in poorer-quality ethical reasoning. Unfortunately, this result does not bode well for the possibility of eliminating or reducing racism, because most people learn about another person's race by seeing it, not reading or hearing about it.

Of course, this does not mean that race is the only driving force behind ethical reasoning; many other explanations are possible, including one uncovered in this study—the story issue. Story issue was important in this study, but somewhat less important than race. And, interestingly, there was no combined effect of race and story issue that affected people's ethical reasoning—in other words, story issue did not appear to make an already bad situation worse. One might have expected that exacerbation was possible because other research has shown that some social issues are inextricably bound up with race.

This study showed that race does matter when people make ethical decisions. Furthermore, that influence should not be minimized in favor of some other reason, such as story issue. This kind of "excuse making" to rationalize the subconscious influence of race is what is called *modern racism*, by which stereotyping is so subtle that people deny the racial component (Entman, 1990). As this study has shown, social issue does matter. Other things may also matter. But so does race. Furthermore, both social issues and race matter independently of each other. Both effects are real.

This chapter suggests that race is another factor that journalists must take into account when they are making ethical decisions. This will hardly come as news to professionals who have been working on the issue for decades. What is news is how subtle and pervasive racism remains. Although some scholars think racial stereotypes are invoked automatically, others are actively pursing research into how people can become aware of these tendencies and take steps to counteract them (Bargh, 1999; Devine & Monteith, 1999).

Counteracting this apparently unthinking human tendency is crucial, because race remains one of the most America's most enduring problems. If journalists' ethical reasoning about some groups of people is of lower quality than it is about others, then the negative portraits of those groups in the media will persist. The media are responsible for racial portrayals that, by virtue of their subtlety, are today even more sinister than was the overt racism of the past (Entman, 1992, 1994). Such portrayals reinforce racial stereotypes in all of society and make the elimination of racism in favor of tolerance, open-mindedness, equality, and universal justice—all of which describe the principled stages of ethical reasoning—an increasingly elusive goal.

CHAPTER 7

The Ethics of Journalistic Deception

Seow Ting Lee
Illinois State University

DEFINITIONS AND PHILOSOPHICAL APPROACHES

"Hello, I am John Smith. I'm calling from police headquarters."

These simple words, when uttered by a journalist making a phone call at a police station, are truthful and deceptive. John Smith is making a true statement to initiate a false belief for the purpose of obtaining information for a story—possibly a very important story. Is this wrong?

It depends. Deception is an illusive and difficult issue. As the inverse of truthtelling, deception is wrong and yet systemic in human relationships, from little white lies in social intercourse to the more capacious deception in the political arena or warfare. Studies have shown that at least one out of four conversations contains some form of deception (Buller & Burgoon, 1996; DePaulo et al., 1996). On the other hand, truthtelling is perhaps the closest to a universal value that we have. According to Mieth (1997), truth is a basic norm, although people "invoke at one moment the norm of truthfulness and at the next moment the right to lie, depending on circumstances and context" (p. 87).

In journalism, with its emphasis on pursuing and publishing truth, deception hits at the heart of the profession, although many journalists and media scholars would consider deception a necessary evil (e.g., Kieran, 1997; Lambeth, 1992). As noted by Kieran (1997), "Paradoxically, we demand that journalists tell the truth, and yet, to get at the truth, they may have to lie" (p. 66).

Deceptive practices by journalists are not uncommon, as seen in 18th-century hoaxes and 19th-century impersonations by muckrakers, and in more recent cases of hidden cameras and fabrication. Benjamin Franklin— "Amer-

92

ica's first great hoaxer"—used fabrication to educate readers. Franklin's "A Witch Trial at Mount Holly," published in *The Pennsylvania Gazette* on October 22, 1730, was aimed at ridiculing Americans who believed in witchcraft. In 1887, *New York World* reporter Elizabeth Conran, who used the byline "Nellie Bly," faked insanity to enter a mental asylum on Blackwell's Island. Her reports, headlined "Ten Days in a Madhouse," detailed the shocking conditions suffered by inmates. According to McCombs, Shaw, and Grey (1976), Bly's reports helped reform the New York mental health care system. Although Bly is often credited as the first American journalist to employ deception in newsgathering, Olasky (1988) documented an earlier case involving undercover reporting on abortion. Olasky suggested that the report triggered stronger media coverage of the physicians who performed abortions and resulted in tighter anti-abortion laws. Like most journalists who used deception, St. Clair and his editor, Louis Jennings, defended the deception as one that was carried out for a noble end.

The noble end defense, however, did not find much favor with Pulitzer board members who questioned the ethics of *Chicago Sun-Times'* Mirage Bar sting operation. In 1977, the *Sun-Times* bought a tavern, rigged it with plumbing and electrical problems, set up reporters as bartenders, and put photographers in hidden rooms to document payoffs to city inspectors. Despite winning some acclaim, the series lost the Pulitzer Prize because judges considered the deception unbecoming of journalists. Unbecoming or otherwise, deception played a significant role in uncovering the Watergate scandal. In *All the Presidents Men* (1974), Washington Post journalists Carl Bernstein and Bob Woodward detailed how they extracted information from an informant, Deep Throat, by falsely telling him that other sources had already provided the information. Another example of journalistic deception is the ABC–Food Lion case. In 1992, ABC "PrimeTime Live" reporters went undercover to expose unhygienic meat processing practices at supermarket chain Food Lion. Not only did the ABC reporters conceal their identities, they also fabricated resumes to get jobs as meat handlers in Food Lion.

These cases of journalistic deception, and many more, demonstrate the vulnerability of journalists when confronted with a desire to get a story, especially in the pursuit of a larger public good. Typically, journalists who use deception rely on utilitarian reasoning—notwithstanding its problems—by considering the consequences of a deceptive act valuable enough to override the harm inflicted on a few.

The main weakness of utilitarianism is its simplistic calculation of risk and benefit, which is vulnerable to uncertainty and imprecision.

Utilitarianism implies that a lie and a truthful statement that achieve the same utility are equal, but we know a lie is negatively weighted to begin with. Often, it is difficult for a person to remain objective when evaluating the consequences of his or her decision to deceive or not to deceive. Besides the temptation to benefit oneself, the use of utilitarianism reasoning to evaluate the rightness of a deceptive act contradicts the notion of test of publicity. Deception must be executed in secrecy, or it would be ineffective.

Arguably, journalistic deception is sometimes necessary for fulfilling the media's watchdog role, and for bringing journalists closer to the truth. However, in the long run, such techniques invariably undermine media credibility. Bok (1978/1989), in her seminal work *Lying*, called these journalistic practices, including those used by Watergate reporters, "lies for the public good" (p. 174). Although such practices stem from an altruistic desire to advance public good, when carried out without thoroughgoing reflection they do serious damage to the profession's standards and the public image. Any small act of deception has a larger significance. As Bok pointed out, "[T]rust in some degree of veracity is the foundation of relations among humans; when this trust shatters or wears away, institutions collapse" (p. 31). German philosopher Immanuel Kant, who devoted considerable effort to outlining his objections to lying, took a deontological (duty-based) approach in suggesting that the moral rightness of an action depends on the act rather than its consequences. The Kantian perspective of truthtelling as a duty without exception offers important insights as to the potential damage inflicted by lies and deception, not only on society at large but also on the liar's human dignity.

Public confidence in news media is at an all-time low today. Surveys show that Americans distrust the news media and have serious misgivings about journalists. Although the distrust in media may be difficult to isolate from the public's loss of faith in all major institutions, veracity is a fundamental given in the field of communications. More specifically for journalism, audience members must believe what they read, hear, or see in the news media, or the design of journalism as the Fourth Estate fails, and fails miserably.

This chapter addresses the question of whether journalists, cushioned by utilitarian motives and a do-gooder spirit, perceive journalistic deception to be wrong. What are the factors that impact journalists' assessment of deception? Before these questions can be answered, we need to understand the concept of journalistic deception.

WHAT IS JOURNALISTIC DECEPTION?

Buller and Burgoon (1996) defined a deceptive message in interpersonal communication as one "knowingly transmitted by a sender to foster a false belief or conclusion by the receiver" (p. 204). According to Bok (1978/1989), a lie is any intentional deceptive message that is stated and that gives power to the liar. Kant described a lie as any intentional statement that is untrue. Inherent in these definitions of deception is the concept of intent. To deceive, you first set out to mislead someone. As explained by Bok, the question of whether you lied or not cannot be answered by establishing the veracity of your statement. The concepts of truth and truthfulness may overlap but they are not alike.

The definition of journalistic deception, however, is far from clear. The phenomenon can take many forms, from outright lying to deceiving, misleading, misrepresenting or merely being less than forthright in words and actions that cause someone else to believe what is untrue (Black, Steele, & Barney, 1997). Some suggest there are three types of journalistic deception (Goodwin & Smith, 1994). The first is *active deception*, which refers to reporters staging events to expose wrongdoing or using hidden cameras and microphones; the second is *misrepresentation*, or reporters impersonating nonreporters—doctors, policemen, victims' kin, and so on; and the third category is *passive deception*, by which reporters allow themselves to be taken for members of the public. A good example is the case of the food reviewer who does not reveal his or her identity at a restaurant.

Typically, the literature focuses on deceptive newsgathering practices such as hidden cameras, impersonation, and sting operations (see Black, Steele, & Barney, 1997; Kieran, 1997; Lambeth, 1992; Weaver & Wilhoit, 1986, 1996). The preoccupation with deception as a newsgathering issue can be traced to the notion that journalists are less likely to fabricate their work than to deceive to get information. According to Christians, Fackler, Rotzoll, and Brittain Mckee (1997), deception rarely occurs in the newswriting phase, but deception in newsgathering is "a persistent temptation, because it often facilitates the process of securing information" (p. 53).

However, a discussion of journalistic deception cannot be confined to active newsgathering techniques. Journalists sometimes lie in their stories to protect their sources, or misrepresent their motives to get that critical interview. Journalists who resort to fabrication, plagiarism, quote tampering, photo manipulation, and staging are knowingly transmitting deceptive messages to foster false beliefs among readers and viewers. Even the practice of flattering a source is problematic; insincere empathy is a serious form of deception practiced by journalists (Elliot, 1989).

The key objection to fabrication in its many forms is rooted in the notion of truthtelling—to the audience—as a fundamental news value. In 1981, *The Washington Post*'s Janet Cooke won a Pulitzer Prize for her story about Jimmy, an 8-year-old heroin addict, only to return the award and lose her job after it was discovered that Jimmy did not exist. In 1998, *Boston Globe* columnist Patricia Smith was sacked for inventing people and quotes in her columns. The *New Republic* fired reporter Stephen Glass for fabricating all or part of 27 articles and using phony notes. Popular *Boston Globe* columnist Mike Barnicle was forced to resign following charges of plagiarism. (Barnicle has since found work at MSNBC, perhaps suggesting that the broadcast industry is more forgiving.) In 2003, the fallout over the Jayson Blair scandal reached dizzying heights at *The New York Times*, widely considered to be America's newspaper of record and one of the world's most influential publications. The *Times* found that Blair fabricated quotes, stole materials from other newspapers, and lied about his whereabouts over a 7-month period.

Fabrication is but one aspect of journalistic deception. It is not uncommon to find journalists withholding information in crime stories to avoid interfering with police investigations. During the Gulf War, some American newspapers reported on amphibious training that turned out to be a case of strategic deception. The amphibious landing did not occur, but the media coverage lured Iraqi forces into erroneous positions. Many reporters knew the exercise was a deception, but did not report that fact. Harris (1992) observed how the U.S. military used the media to help the coalition cause and to confuse the Iraqis. For example, to dampen Iraqi morale and boost defections, the CIA planted a false story about the defection of 60 Iraqi tanks (p. 154).

The definition of journalistic deception is incomplete without considering the nature of deception, which can occur by omission or by commission. The former refers to any act that omits significant information with the intention to initiate or sustain a false belief. The latter is an act that involves active or deliberate altering of information. Bok (1978/1989) distinguished between lies and deception by viewing a lie as an intentional deceptive message that is stated, unlike deception that is a broader concept: "When we undertake to deceive others intentionally, we communicate messages meant to mislead them, meant to make them believe what we ourselves do not believe" (p. 13). Gert (1988) argued that moral rule prohibiting deception is often stated erroneously as "don't lie." Gert asserted that, as a rule, "don't lie" is inadequate because: "A rational person would want to be avoid being led to have false belief by silence, by gesture, even by a true statement made in a certain tone of voice; it is being led to have a false belief that is important, not that it was done by making a false statement. Thus the rule should be concerned with prohibiting acts so as to lead someone to have a false belief. I shall formulate this rule as 'Don't deceive' " (p. 126).

The distinction between deception by commission and deception by omission was captured in Elliot and Culver's (1992) comprehensive definition of journalistic deception: an act to communicate messages, verbally (lie) or nonverbally through the withholding of information with the intention to initiate or sustain a false belief. Elliot and Culver maintained that some forms of deception through omission may be more problematic than lies, although the former does not contain a property of assertion. In response to those who suggested that lying is worse than other types of deception (Chisholm & Freehan, 1977; Freid, 1978), they offered this example: Lying to a stranger on an airplane about the price of a laptop seems less egregious than a doctor not telling a patient about the side effects of a drug.

By all accounts, deception, with its intricate moral dimensions, is a phenomenon that occurs habitually in human interaction. Yet, it is an important theme underlying many of the ethical conundrums in journalism. Weaver and Wilhoit (1996), in their 1992 national survey of American journalists, asked respondents to consider 10 questionable reporting scenarios: disclosing confidential sources, using false identification, paying for confidential information, badgering sources, using personal documents without consent, using unauthorized confidential documents, undercover reporting, using hidden cameras and microphones, using recreation of news events, and disclosing the names of rape victims. Four of the scenarios— false identification, undercover reporting, hidden cameras, and recreation of news events (staging)—involved journalistic deception.

Although philosophical discussion of the problem is robust, scholars have little other than anecdotal evidence to gauge the pervasiveness of the practice. One rare effort was Luljak's (2000) participant observation study at an unnamed Midwestern television station. Based on 14 hours of fieldwork, Lujlak concluded that journalistic deception was casual and routine to the extent that journalists did not even think of it as deception. Routine practices include journalists lying about their identities, suppressing information that would embarrass sources, bantering insincerely with sources, and broadcasting false information as favors to police.

WHAT JOURNALISTS SAY ABOUT DECEPTION

The following discussion of journalistic deception is based on a Web-conducted survey and depth interviews with journalists from the IRE (Investigative Reporters and Editors, Inc.) in 2002. Between February 2 and February 23, the survey generated 740 responses, or a response rate of 19.4%. Although the IRE had 4,370 members in February 2002, the survey was delivered successfully to 3,795 e-mail addresses. Whereas this response rate is less than optimal for professionwide generalization, it represents the largest survey of this sort on a single ethical issue of working journalists. Furthermore, when examined in the context of studies of journalist's moral development as well as the existing literature, the responses indicate both the depth and subtlety of professional thinking about this central issue.

Of the 740 survey respondents, 42.3% were female and 57.7% were male. Most of the respondents were Caucasian (88.5%); 2.8% were African American; 3.5% were Hispanics; 2.4% were Asians; .1% were Native American; and 2.6% were "Other." The respondents' mean age was 40 and the median was 39. Their news careers ranged from 1 to 49 years, with a average of 15.8 years in the profession. More than half (59.5%) worked for newspapers. Television journalists (14.2%) were the second largest group. The rest worked for magazines, radio, Web-based media, and wire services, and a small number of "other" (media research departments, alternative weeklies, and media outlets based in journalism schools). The news organizations they worked for employed an average of 230 full-time journalists, and a median of 100. More than half of the respondents (55.5%) worked for a news organization owned by a chain or group. Nearly 90% of the respondents had a bachelor's degree, and 43% had a higher degree / coursework. About 41% had an undergraduate degree in journalism / mass communication, and 14% had a double major that included journalism / mass communication. About 70% had completed a college-level class in media ethics or journalism ethics. More than half (57.6%) worked for a news organization that had an official code of ethics. A smaller number (17.3%) worked for a news organization that employed a full-time or part-time ombudsman.

In summary, the respondents were not journalism neophytes. Their demographic profile shows a sample of experienced journalists working in large news organizations. This profile is similar to the one of journalists who completed the DIT. Again, it is important to note that although this survey was not random, the demographic profile of the respondents is consistent with the other profiles reviewed in chapter 3.

Depth interviews were conducted between February 7 and March 6, 2002, with 20 reporters and editors who volunteered for interviews through the survey. Depth interviews are useful for understanding a journalist's perspective and for probing accounts of deceptive behavior. The 20 interviewees worked for newspapers of all sizes, magazines, weeklies, wire services, local television stations, networks, and Web-based media. The longest news career of those interviewed was 30 years, and the shortest was 4 years.

ASSESSMENT OF JOURNALISTIC DECEPTION

Charting the Terrain: 16 Deceptive Practices

In the Web-based survey, respondents evaluated 16 deceptive practices on a seven-point scale, from "not at all justified" to "very justified" based on the question, "Given an important story that is of vital public interest, would the following be justified?"

The results show that these journalists considered some practices more deceptive than others, consistent with literature that suggests people judge deception on a continuum of good to bad.

The practice of "making a statement that is untrue to readers/viewers" was almost unanimously rejected; 99% of respondents rated the practice as "not at all justified" or "mostly" not justified. Two other rejected practices were: "using nonexistent characters and quotes in a story" (97%) and "altering quotes" (96%). However, when it came to withholding information from a source, only 9.8% of respondents indicated that the practice is not at all or mostly not justified.

The journalists in the sample rejected the 16 deceptive practices in the following order:

Making an untrue statement to readers/viewers.
Using nonexistent characters or quotes in a story.
Altering quotes.
Altering photographs.
Publishing or airing information that you know exists but have no
　　access to or cannot verify yet.
Recreating a news event (staging).
Making an untrue statement to sources.
Providing misleading or false attribution to protect a source.

Claiming to be someone else.
Putting a positive spin on a story to make it more interesting.
Withholding information from readers / viewers.
Recording sound or image without the interviewee's /
    newsmaker's knowledge.
Getting employed in a firm or organization to get inside information.
Misrepresenting motives by flattering a source or showing
    empathy to get information.
Using hidden cameras and microphones.
Withholding information from sources.

Based on this ranking, at least two patterns were evident. Respondents reacted more favorably to deceptive practices targeting news sources than to those targeting news audiences. For example, nearly 40% of the respondents rejected the practice of withholding information from the audience (21.6% "not all justified"; 17.7% "mostly not justified"), compared to fewer than 10% of respondents rejecting the practice of withholding information from news sources (4.5% "not at all justified"; 5.3% "mostly not justified"). Similarly, nearly 99% of respondents rejected the practice of making an untrue statement to the audience (96.1% "not at all justified"; 2.6% "mostly not justified"), compared to the 80% of respondents who rejected the practice of making an untrue statement to news sources (63% "not at all justified"; 17.3% "mostly not justified").

In general, respondents also were more approving of deceptive practices that involved omission (withholding information; surreptitious recording of information) than of deceptive practices involving commission (impersonation, lying, tampering with or falsifying information).

The 16 deceptive practices were presented to respondents sans context. The next part of the survey attempted to ascertain whether context would matter. A deceptive practice was inserted into five scenarios: impersonation (steakhouse), lying to a source (campaign finance), hidden cameras (nursing home), fabricating a story (FBI), and withholding a story (Special Forces). The nursing home case was identical to that used in the DIT study and is reproduced elsewhere in this volume.

ISSUES IN CONTEXT: RESPONSES TO SCENARIOS

Context itself makes a direct comparison among the scenarios difficult. However, the results are consistent with the pattern of responses to the 16 deceptive practices.

The five scenarios, described in Table 7.1, elicited between 4.9% and 70.5% of strong rejection ("not at all justified"). The FBI scenario (70.5%) topped the list, followed by steakhouse (47.8%), campaign finance (29.3%), nursing home (5.3%), and Special Forces (4.9%). In terms of strong approval ("very justified"), the nursing home scenario gathered the highest rating (50.5%), followed by Special Forces (24.2%), campaign finance (8.0%), steakhouse (5.0%), and FBI (3.2%).

The journalists were more approving of the use of hidden cameras in the nursing home than the use of impersonation in the steakhouse scenario. Impersonation, according to Elliot (1989), is the most insidious and morally problematic of all deceptive newsgathering methods because the journalist is pretending to be someone he or she is not for the sole purpose of getting a story. The illegality of impersonating certain public officials also adds bite to the point. Inherent in impersonation is the element of deception by commission.

TABLE 7.1

The IRE Scenarios

Scenario 1

Reporter Jane Smith receives a tip-off that a popular local steakhouse is serving old meat. Although there have been no cases of food poisoning so far, the old meat is a potential public health hazard. To get evidence of wrongdoing, Smith applies for the position of assistant to the chef, by creating a fake resume claiming extensive experience working in restaurants. Is it justifiable for Smith to go undercover and impersonate a steakhouse employee?

Scenario 2

Newspaper reporter Alan Meyer gets an anonymous phone call from a person who claims newly elected Governor Shawn Williams received illegal contributions amounting to $400,000 from a large real-estate company. The caller refuses to meet Meyer but suggests he talk to a local businessman who helped launder the money. At first, the businessman denies the allegations. However, when Meyer tells him he has witnesses and documents to prove the case (when in fact he doesn't), the person agrees to cooperate if he is not identified in the story. Was it justifiable for Meyer to lie to the businessman?

Scenario 3

This scenario is identical to the hidden camera dilemma in the DIT survey of professional journalists reviewed in chapters 3 and 4.

(continued)

TABLE 7.1   (continued)

Scenario 4

The editors at Big Moon Times have information that the FBI has traced a group of suspects to their town. These suspects are believed to have sent a letter that contained anthrax spores to a network TV station in New York City. It is also believed the suspects may have biological weapons at their disposal and may use them if confronted. Rumors of the FBI's arrival in the town are circulating. To buy time and divert the suspects' attention, the FBI requests the newspaper's assistance in planting a fake story to say the town is not being targeted and that FBI agents are searching other distant towns and are already moving to adjacent states looking for the suspects. Is it justifiable for the editors to publish the story?

Scenario 5

Newspaper reporter Richard Flink has information that U.S. Special Forces have left their base in North Carolina for a secret mission to nab members of a terrorist network and its leader hiding in Somalia. When Flink approaches Major General Bill Davidson to verify the information, the Major General denies the plan exists. However, Flink has sources domestic and abroad that confirm U.S. Special Forces officers have been spotted in neighboring Kenya. When Flink decides to write the story, the Major General and the Assistant Defense Secretary call the paper to tell Flink the operation is actually in place but they ask him to withhold the story for the safety of the U.S. military personnel involved in the mission. Is it justifiable for the newspaper to withhold the story?

In contrast, deception by commission is weaker in the case of hidden cameras, which many journalists would consider to be a guileless, objective tool of information gathering. Conceivably, the nature of the information gathered— wrongdoing against defenseless victims in the nursing home scenario—is another persuasive factor.

Compared to the other scenarios, the campaign finance scenario, which involved a journalist lying to a crooked source, shows the least distinctive pattern of response. Respondents, although showing some disapproval, were more divided. This scenario is an attempt to test Bok's concept of "lying to liars." A separate question on the questionnaire also asked respondents to evaluate the statement, "It is more acceptable to lie to or deceive a source if he or she is a dishonest person." Although respondents mostly rejected the statement, it is debatable whether the question, worded in a direct and pointed way, generated candid responses from respondents.

Interviews with journalists showed that many journalists believed it is more acceptable to deceive someone who is a bad person, especially as an excuse to justify deception. As one noted, it is more acceptable to lie to Osama bin Laden than to a Sunday school teacher. Many journalists justify deceptive methods as a reasonable means of going after the "bad guys." One respondent said, "When you get down and deal with pigs, you get a little mud on you."

Comparing the responses to the two scenarios (FBI and Special Forces) related to the September 11, 2001, terrorist attacks, journalists said withholding a story was less egregious than fabricating a story. The FBI scenario, which involved journalists fabricating a story to mislead terrorists and aid law enforcement activities, generated the strongest disapproval among the five scenarios.

Implicit in this result is a qualitative and moral distinction between deception by omission and deception by commission. To the journalists in this study, the act of withholding a story was an omission that was less problematic morally than publishing a false story, notwithstanding the good that can be achieved by both acts. The omission–commission distinction was also supported by the response pattern to the 16 deceptive practices.

Several of the journalists interviewed maintained that only acts involving outright falsification of information could be viewed as "lying" or "deception." To these journalists, it was not deceptive (wrong) for a reporter to withhold her identity, unlike the case of the reporter telling someone that she is a doctor. Hence, it was natural for the journalists to offer nonidentification as a morally sound alternative to impersonation and fake resumes. As one journalist put it, "It's okay if you don't tell people who you are, but you cannot put on a doctor's jacket and pose as a doctor, or tell people, 'Hey, I am a lawyer.' "

In summary, the responses revealed a scheme of moral reasoning based on three domains:

- Who is being deceived: News audiences or newsmakers/sources?
- What is the perceived moral character of the person deceived?
- What is the nature of the deceptive act: commission or omission?

As a result, these journalists were more tolerant of hidden cameras, nonidentification, lying to sources, and withholding a story than of fabrication, impersonation, photo manipulation, quote tampering, or staging. They carefully distinguished between deceptive acts aimed at news audiences and those targeting news sources, considering the latter to be less deserving of truth. Few journalists were willing to breach the implicit contract between journalists and their audiences, consistent with the literature that focuses on the role of journalism as an impartial and truthful purveyor of information.

To the journalists in this study who relied on utilitarian reasoning to justify deception, newsmakers and news sources were merely means to an end, the end being the fulfillment of a responsibility to news audiences. This unequal treatment is questionable considering that the two groups are not mutually exclusive. By treating one group poorly, journalists risk alienating all.

Second, the journalists were more tolerant of deception aimed at wrongdoers. In interviews, journalism's moral authority was expressed in a sense of reciprocity or "an eye for an eye" justification. Deception was often viewed as an appropriate strategy for dealing with difficult newsmakers, especially as a way to extract information that would have been impossible to obtain otherwise. One newspaper reporter declared that she would not lose too much sleep over deceiving "someone who is intentionally hurting other people." To many of the journalists, Enron executives were fair game, suggesting that moral judgment was being cast, a finding that is consistent with other scholarship about investigative reporters.

Clearly, to these journalists, moral judgment was an integral aspect of newswork. For some, deception was part of a strategy to level a perceived power imbalance. Journalists revealed a preconceived notion of who is bad and who is good. Politicians, judges, and executives were deemed to have a smaller claim to the truth than were the single mother, the blue- collar worker, or the less powerful and less media-savvy segments of society. This notion has been shaped by journalism's social surveillance function and journalists' innate distrust of institutions and officials. However, as earlier chapters have demonstrated, an overdependence on preconceived notions (stereotyping) can be dangerous. People typically consider others to be less ethical than themselves (Price, 1973), but there is no evidence to suggest that journalists are better than others in judging moral character.

Second, journalists may deploy deception as an act of reciprocity but research shows that few people accurately judge whether they have been deceived (Ekman, 2001). The ensuing double standard is remarkable. When dealing with newsmakers, these journalists relied on a utilitarian calculus of harm and benefit (it's okay to lie to those I believe are lying to me), but when it came to news audiences, they were guided by a Kantian or nonab-solutist perspective that rejected all deception.

Finally, the journalists considered deception by commission to be more egregious than was deception by omission. There are explanations for this outlook (Ekman, 2001). It is easier to conceal than to falsify; chances of being caught are lower because a person does not need to work out a fictional story in advance. And unlike falsification, concealment is passive, and hence in-volves less guilt. When caught, a person can rely on a number of excuses: ig-norance, memory lapse, or an intention to reveal the information later.

In sum, the journalistic deception continuum is shaped by three princi-ples: evaluations of the target audience, the moral character of victims, and the omission–commission distinction. A single deceptive act appears as a point on a continuum of justifiable-to-reprehensible professional deception.

Consistent with the survey results, the journalists interviewed consid-ered some deceptive practices to be more acceptable than others. Fabrica-tion, photo manipulation, quote tampering, and impersonation were considered more egregious than were flattering or lying to a source or newsmaker. A newspaper reporter has this to say about fabrication and flattery: "A credible journalist would never in a million years think of fab-ricating a story. That's the cardinal—you just don't do that. But everyone flatters sources, or they should be." Hidden cameras were evaluated on a case-by-case basis.

The act of flattering a source or demonstrating insincere empathy to gain information was not only highly tolerated but also appreciated, as journalists expressed an admiration for colleagues who could charm their way to a good story. Although flattery or insincere empathy was valued, the journalists were quick to draw the line at fawning or any act that may compromise their presumed sense of objectivity; for example, romantic entanglements with sources or personal involvement in a fundraiser for a newsmaker.

Because the journalists in this study showed marked patterns in evaluat-ing journalistic deception, the question then became what might influence that assessment.

Influences of Tolerance of Deception

Previous chapters have reviewed the research on individual influences on moral decision making (e.g., Singletary et al., 1990; Voakes, 1997; Weaver & Wilhoit, 1986, 1996). Most research, however, has found that external influ-ences (e.g., organizational pressures, professional values, and routines of work) outweigh the individual or internal variables. In this survey, 38 variables were considered as potential factors influencing tolerance of journalistic deception. A regression analysis based on four ordinary least squares (OLS) regression models (Table 7.2) shows that, in general, external factors (see organizational model) are better predictors of tolerance of journalistic deception than are individual-level variables. In sum, tolerance of deception is shaped mainly on the job, as a function of organizational factors and newsroom pressures, consistent with the literature (Beam, 1993; Borden, 2000; Bowers, 1998; Breed, 1955; Singletary et al., 1990; Valenti, 1998; Voakes, 1997; Weaver & Wilhoit, 1996; Westbrook, 1995; Wulfemeyer, 1990).

Individual journalists encounter much resistance in their attempts to bypass organizational control and business and resource constraints, as shown in Breed's (1955) classic study of social control in the newsroom. Under the exigencies of the real world, ideals and behavior often diverge. In the corporate world and in the military, organizational structures helped legitimize unethical acts to the extent of pushing employees into behaving unethically (James, 1982). In journalism, newsroom pressures encouraging deception are widespread despite the presence of codes of ethics and media lawyers. One of the journalists interviewed, a newspaper editor, narrated how editors resisted official codes of behavior and pushed reporters into committing deceptive practices:

> You know, there have been situations over the years—I won't say what papers it has happened at, but I have gotten a feeling that an editor was suggesting, "We absolutely will not back you up on this if you're caught—wink wink." It was like, "Go as far as you want to get the story but we're going to leave you out to dry. We are officially saying that this is not something that we condone." But you can feel in the editor's tone that "If you're a really good reporter, you wouldn't care what I think."

In this sample of journalists, competition and medium emerged as the two most salient predictors of tolerance of deception, underscoring the importance of organizational influences in shaping ethical judgment.

Competition and Medium

Competition is the most important predictor of deception tolerance. Journalists who rated more highly the importance of competition as a consideration in ethical judgment were more likely to tolerate journalistic deception, a finding that has much support in the academic literature (e.g., Bagdikian, 2000; Borden & Pritchard, 1997; McChesney, 1997). Increasingly, bottom-line pressures shape journalistic practices as well as news con-

TABLE 7.2

Regression Analysis of Predictors of Deception Tolerance (β, *N* = 740)

Predictor Variables	Personal Model	Organizational Model	Mixed Model	Full Model
1. Age	−.079	—	—	−.039
2. Gender	.078	—	.134*	.114
3. Race (Caucasian v. Non-Caucasian)	.008	—	—	.051
4. Journalism experience (years)	−.074	—	—	.006
5. Education (years)	.069	—	—	.022
6. Journalism major	.033	—	—	.042
7. Taken college-level journalism class	−.004	—	.068	.048
8. Taken media ethics class	−.043	—	−.116	−.042
9. Attendance of religious services	−.028	—	−.063	−.066
10. Political leaning	.015	—	—	−.051
11. Income	.058	—	—	−.072
12. U.S. citizenship	−.119**	—	−.119*	−.092
13. Influence: religion/personal values	.038	—	—	.075
14. Influence: journalism educators	−.077	—	—	−.077
15. Medium (print vs. TV)	—	−.271***	−.289***	−.381***
16. Supervisory role	—	−.063	−.083	−.018
17. Organization size	—	.042	−.107*	.048
18. Owned by a public corporation	—	−.095	—	−.134
19. Majority of shares publicly traded	—	.080	.035	.071
20. Chain ownership	—	.010	—	−.007
21. Code of ethics	—	−.018	—	−.023
22. Ombudsman	—	−.030	—	.025
23. Adversary role conception	—	−.107	−.108	−.177*
24. Disseminator role conception	—	−.153**	−.152**	−.128
25. Interpretive role conception	—	.127*	.126*	.130
26. Populist role conception	—	.117*	.133*	.102
27. Influence: peers/colleagues	−.058	—	.065	
28. Influence: editors, news editors	—	−.107	—	−.021
29. Influence: code of ethics	—	−.035	—	−.040
30. Influence: publishers, owners	—	−.051	—	−.061
31. Influence: advertisers	—	−.003	—	−.030
32. Influence: relationship with source	—	−.043	—	−.001
33. Influence: protection of source	—	.081	—	.046
34. Influence: competition	—	.361***	.298***	.329***
35. Influence: public opinion and image	—	−.016	—	−.034

(continued)

TABLE 7.2   (*continued*)

Predictor Variables	Personal Model	Organizational Model	Mixed Model	Full Model
36. Influence: ombudsman	—	.022	—	.035
37. Influence: audience's reaction	—	.032	—	.040
38. Influence: legality	—	−.125*	−.126*	.112
Intercept	63.623	72.763	77.035	83.283
F	1.995*	3.615***	7.549***	2.768***
R-square	.045	.235	.284	.324
Adjusted R-square	.023	.170	.246	.207

*$p < .05$; ** $p < .01$; *** $p < .001$

tent. In interviews, competition emerged as a key motivator of deception. Although the journalists assigned an instrumental value to journalistic deception (as a strategy for getting important information when all means have been exhausted, handling difficult newsmakers, protecting news sources, facilitating objectivity, or acting in self-defense), many conceded that deception was often motivated by "pure laziness." Convenience, cost, deadlines, and a desire to get a competitive edge over others in the business helped push journalists to use hidden cameras, tamper with quotes, fabricate characters and quotes, manipulate photographs, hide their identities, or impersonate a nonjournalist.

One journalist noted:

> The primary focus from above, meaning our bosses, is not, "Let's talk about ethical and journalistic considerations as the most important overriding factor that pertain to us in this particular story." The focus is we need to do a compelling story that is going to get lots of attention and grab viewers. A whole lot of the time, the two things conflict, and they conflict a lot.

The second most important predictor of deception tolerance is medium. Television journalists were more tolerant of journalistic deception than were their print colleagues. Not only were the television journalists in this sample more tolerant of hidden cameras, they were also more tolerant of other deceptive practices.

As a medium that is low in interactivity and engagement compared to print, television's programming is driven by visual impact, another finding that has some support in the literature (Paterno, 1998; Weaver & Wilhoit 1996; Weinberg , 1997; Wulfemeyer, 1990). That tolerance for many sorts of deception would vary by medium of employment is reasonable, considering that a deceptive practice rarely works alone. The demands of television may push its journalists to use hidden cameras but, to be successful, hidden cameras must be accompanied by other deceptive practices such as impersonation and lying to sources or newsmakers.

Interestingly, what emerged from the interviews was a deep-seated conviction, especially among print journalists, that television journalists use more deception. The print journalists, who used varying degrees of diplomacy to suggest that television journalists also tend to be less ethical, conceded that television journalists face a different set of pressures. These statements about television journalists were provocative and controversial but, from the survey data, there was evidence to suggest that television journalists were more tolerant of journalistic deception than were print journalists. It cannot be concluded, however, that television journalists are less ethical than their print colleagues.

Legality and Journalistic Role Conception

Although competition and medium are the most important predictors of tolerance of journalistic deception, several other variables are also important. From the regression analysis discussed earlier, legality and journalistic role conception are reasonably good predictors of tolerance of journalistic deception.

Survey respondents who rated higher the importance of legality as a consideration in ethical decision making were less tolerant of journalistic deception, consistent with the notion that legal concerns may have a chilling effect on journalists' work (Borden & Pritchard, 1997; Kirtley, 2000; Paterno, 1998; Voakes, 1998). The issue of legality also emerged in the interviews; many of the journalists interviewed were concerned about legality, but some quickly connected the idea of legal troubles to the bottom line. Journalists who were more concerned about legal issues were more cautious about the use of deceptive practices, many of which carry legal implications.

Whereas journalistic thinking about deception was clearly connected to the practices in individual newsrooms and the context of particular media markets, how journalists define their professional worldview—what the literature refers to as *roles*—has also been suggested as a possible influence on ethical thinking. The survey asked journalists to specify their roles using role conception definitions adopted from Weaver and Wilhoit's 1986 survey that built on work of Johnstone et al. (1976). Those roles are:

- *Disseminator journalists* get information to the public quickly, reaching the widest audience possible, and avoiding stories with unverifiable facts. As more or less neutral bystanders, these journalists are less likely to be involved in the pursuit of in-depth stories.
- *Interpretive journalists* are grounded in three roles: investigating government claims, analyzing and interpreting complex problems, and discussing public policies.
- *Populist-mobilizers* have four major functions: developing the interests of the public, providing entertainment, setting the political agenda, and letting ordinary people express their views.
- *Adversarial journalists* consider themselves as watchdogs of government and business.

The disseminator role is the most salient predictor of tolerance of deception; these journalists were less tolerant of deception. Disseminators are less likely to encounter situations requiring hidden cameras or other deceptive methods. Implicit in this finding is a relationship between detachment and a rejection of deception, although it is conceivable that tight deadlines could push journalists toward other forms of journalistic deception such as fabrication or quote tampering for the sake of convenience.

Respondents who were more oriented in the interpretive role conception were more tolerant of deception. Again, this finding implies that journalists are more inclined to engage in deceptive acts when they go beyond merely reporting the facts.

Like their interpretive-oriented colleagues, populist-mobilizer journalists in this study were more tolerant of deception. This is also the group of journalists who capture the spirit of public journalism (Weaver & Wilhoit, 1996). This finding is likely to empower critics of public journalism who warn of the slippery slope of overt agenda setting and engagement. An implication is that populist-mobilizers, in their attempts at reform and civic engagement, may cross the line into deceptive behavior—a finding that is certain to generate professional debate because civic journalism is sometimes viewed as competing with investigative journalism for scarce organizational resources.

However, journalists who were more adversarial were less tolerant of deception. This finding is contrary to Weaver and Wilhoit's suggestion that the adversarial role conception is associated with a higher tolerance of unethical newsgathering methods. This variable is worth noting despite its relatively low significance ($\beta = -.177$, $p < .05$; full model) among the four role conceptions. Adversarial journalists are more likely than any other journalists to encounter situations calling for deceptive methods; investigative reporters, in pursuit of the public good, are more likely to abandon their objectivity and other journalistic values to pursue evidence of wrongdoing by officials (Ettema & Glasser, 1998; Glasser & Ettema, 1989).

The adversarial journalist presents a persistent puzzle. It is possible that when faced with a study about ethics, the journalists in this study, as members of a professional organization for investigative reporters and editors, may have adopted a defensive stance. Conversely, the results may reflect a genuine response considering that, more than any other group of journalists, investigative journalists are well aware of criticisms of overzealous and aggressive newsgathering tactics.

The adversary role conception has become a minority mindset among American journalists. Only 20% of the journalists surveyed in 1992 rated "being an adversary of government" as extremely important, compared to the two thirds who said it is extremely important to investigate government claims. Weaver and Wilhoit (1996) noted, "Our finding represents either the ultimate denial, mass lying or a misunderstanding" (p. 140). It would appear that after being inundated with a barrage of criticism from public figures and politicians, journalists today are keen to distance themselves from the term *adversarial* and its negative undertones.

Other Significant Predictors

Worth mentioning are the variables of gender, organization size, and U.S. citizenship. Interestingly, the male journalists in this study were more tolerant of journalistic deception than were female journalists ($\beta = 134$, $p < .05$; mixed model). It is possible that some of these male-centered elements, which are intrinsic in the concept of journalistic deception and its retaliatory and instrumental values, were less appealing to women journalists.

The journalists who were U.S. citizens were more likely to reject journalistic deception than were respondents who were not U.S. citizens ($\beta = .119$, $p < .05$; mixed model). Truthtelling may be a cross-cultural journalistic value (e.g., Cooper et al., 1989; Laitila, 1995), but journalists from different cultures exhibit different attitudinal patterns favoring certain news items over others, despite the common news values of timeliness, novelty, and so on. Truthtelling, as a journalistic value, is shaped by cultural or situational factors, consistent with the literature on interpersonal communication (Buller & Burgoon, 1996; DePaulo et al., 1996; Waisbord, 1996).

Organization size is positively correlated with unethical behavior. In this study, a journalist who worked for a larger news organization was more likely to reject journalistic deception than was a journalist working for a smaller news organization ($\beta = -.107$, $p < .05$; mixed model). Intrinsic in the notion of organization size is resource availability. A larger news organization is likely to have a larger pool of resources that facilitates a stronger commitment to training staff in ethics, writing up official codes of ethics, and hiring ombudsmen, and hence is more likely to foster a stronger awareness of ethical issues.

EDUCATION, OMBUDSMEN, AND CODES OF ETHICS: A LOST CAUSE?

Moral decision making is an untidy and complicated process. Contrary to expectations, some variables that had appeared intuitive were not salient predictors of tolerance of deception. These included variables associated with journalism experience, journalism education, media ethics education, codes of ethics, and ombudsmen. In this study, age and experience do not appear to be important, and contrary to common wisdom—and perhaps of some disappointment to journalism educators—this study found no relationship between a journalist's tolerance of deception and whether he or she had received media ethics instruction, taken a college-level journalism class, or had been a journalism major.

Whether an organization has an ombudsmen or not bears no relationship to a journalist's tolerance of journalistic deception, although several studies have found that journalists who worked in newspapers with ombudsmen are more likely to exercise ethical caution in their work (Luljak, 2000). Similarly, whether an organization has an official code of ethics is not a predictor of a journalist's tolerance of journalistic deception. In the interviews, many journalists questioned the effectiveness of ethics codes, consistent with the literature critical of ethics codes (e.g., Black, 1985; Harris, 1992; Merrill & O'Dell, 1983; Turner, Edgley, & Olmstead, 1975).

Although this finding about codes of ethics may be discouraging, it can be viewed as a positive development. Genuine moral development can occur only when people go beyond a stage of being other-directed by rules to an inner-directed stage of internalized rules. The progression is from a heteronomous stage at which right and wrong are defined externally to an autonomous stage at which reflective judgment is used to assess what is right and wrong, and the meaning and relevance of a rule can be explained and defended. Perhaps the rejection of written codes of ethics is a reflection of this growth.

As observed by many of the journalists, codes may be useful for a young reporter entering the profession, but they are less so for a veteran journalist with years or decades of journalism experience. However, another rule-based approach to morality lies in the legal framework, which appears to be a salient deterrent to the journalists in this study, as discussed earlier in the chapter. These journalists may have rejected codes of ethics but, rightly so, they viewed laws to be a more binding and enforceable set of rules.

CHAPTER 8

Advertising Practitioners Respond: The News Is Not Good

Anne Cunningham
Louisiana State University

Whether it is controversy over the latest Calvin Klein campaign or attacks against R. J. Reynolds' use of the cartoon character Joe Camel, it seems much of the criticism of media falls on its commercial content. Even the Pontifical Council of the Catholic Church (1996) has issued a treatise on ethics in advertising.

Critics have accused advertising of selling cigarettes and alcohol to children, polluting the airwaves and landscapes, unduly influencing the free flow of information through the media, subverting the marketplace, and even undermining personal autonomy. Some go so far as to argue that advertising, by its very nature, is unethical. Ethicist Roger Crisp, for example, asserted, "[I]n a very real sense, decisions are made for consumers by persuasive advertisers, who occupy the motivational territory properly belonging to the agent.... It seems, then, that persuasive advertising does override the autonomy of consumers, and that, if the overriding of autonomy, all things being equal, is immoral, then persuasive advertising is immoral" (Crisp, 1987, pp. 414, 416–417). Although this contention, which essentially relegates consumers to unwitting dupes, is debatable, the criticism itself is widespread. Leveling a more institutional attack on the industry, Sut Jhally (1998) contended that advertising, acting as the "mouthpiece of capitalism," erodes cultural values, leaving in their place the hollow desire for consumption of goods. Both sorts of criticisms by inference implicate individual advertising practitioners in minimally acquiescing to decisions that many others consider to be ethically problematic. Maximally, individual practitioners, again by inference, are indicted as willing participants in an immoral act.

This chapter examines the moral development of those already in advertising. In so doing, this study provides a benchmark for an industry whose professionals have never before been evaluated using the DIT. It provides information on how these advertising professionals evaluate two typical industry dilemmas—each at the root of some of the most essential criticisms of the profession.

ETHICS IN ADVERTISING: PAST RESEARCH

The ethical issues raised in advertising are not entirely different from those raised in other related disciplines: journalism, marketing, and business administration. Advertising, however, serves a very different societal function—increasing market growth by persuading consumers to purchase products—than journalism, which aims to inform. These dissimilar objectives necessarily lead to some different types of ethical questions.

Christians' (1980) discussion of journalistic ethics showed that journalists and advertisers face many of the same constraints. Deadline pressures as well as the economic structure of the media and the drive for profits constrain a journalist's autonomy. Without autonomy, there is no personal responsibility for ethical decisions. Although members of both professions face these economic and temporal constraints, advertisers' very mission is to generate profits for their clients by persuading consumers. Journalists, on the other hand, are charged with selling newspapers (or attracting viewers) by providing useful, interesting information.

Some of the ethical issues particular to the advertising industry have already been uncovered. Christians (1980) surveyed advertising agency personnel and found that ethical problems fell along two dimensions: the advertising message, which includes questions of what should be advertised, how the message should be crafted, and where ethics enter the process of message construction; and the agency–client relationship, which includes serving both the agency and the client fairly and confidentially. The findings indicated that advertising practitioners think about immediate consequences when deciding how to act. In other words, act utilitarianism is most often used to resolve ethical problems. The researchers argued that a more sophisticated decision-making process based on long-term consequences would be more appropriate. This process would resemble a system of rule utilitarianism, an approach that would allow for some universalization of ethical principles based on long-term outcomes.

Hunt and Chonko (1987) expanded on these findings with a survey of advertising managers. They found a discrepancy between the ethical issues covered by industry codes of ethics and those actually faced by practitioners. Once again, treating clients fairly topped the managers' lists of ethical problems in advertising.

These studies suggest that advertising ethics differ from journalistic ethics, and that the issues encountered by advertising practitioners may be better solved using different ethical constructs. As Martinson (1996) pointed out, the persuasive nature of advertising places an additional burden on advertisers to act responsibly:

> For the advertiser—and advertising students—the question, therefore, must center around making judgments as to which types and methods of persuasion are ethical and which are not. Students need to understand that the key to making such judgments ethically rests with the advertiser placing the concerns of his/her intended audience at the same level as his/her own and those of the client or employer. (Martinson, 1996, p. 12)

Whereas numerous scholarly articles have examined the ethicality of the industry, advertising ethics tends to be marginalized, treated as a special topic rather than an ongoing area of investigation. A 1999 issue of *Journal of Mass Media Ethics* devoted to persuasion ethics represented the spectrum of research generally done in the area. Baker (1999) presented five possible justifications for persuasive communications. Cunningham (1999) examined one particular practice, advertisers' efforts to influence editorial content in magazines, and offered an ethical criticism. Park, Weigold, and Treise (1999) provided a cross-cultural analysis of Americans' and South Koreans' perceptions of advertising ethics. And Tucker and Stout (1999) addressed the moral development of advertising educators.

This research covered a variety of topics, yet suggested few solutions or models by which professionals can better reason through ethics problems. However, the same essential problems remain. Cunningham and Haley (1998) conducted qualitative interviews with advertising professionals to update Christians' earlier work, and found that ethical dilemmas continued to revolve around business practices and client relations. Based on the findings, they suggested stakeholder theory as a model for helping advertisers consider and balance the needs of all parties to a moral problem. This sporadic academic analysis—despite a stability of the ethical problems that practitioners say they face—suggested that both the academy and the profession need to take a serious look at ethical decision making in the field.

No one has examined the moral reasoning abilities of people in the advertising industry. With professionals, scholars, and the public questioning advertising practices and even its raison d'etre, the moral development of its professionals seems to be an appropriate starting point. This study offers such a benchmark. Like the work on journalists reviewed earlier in this volume, this chapter seeks to link moral decision making with other variables in an effort to better understand the industry and the moral growth of those who work in it.

STUDY DESIGN: THE ADVERTISING VARIATION

Using the Defining Issues Test and past research as a starting point, advertising practitioners were asked to respond to the four standard DIT scenarios reviewed in chapter 2, plus two new, advertising-specific dilemmas. The new stories focused on the practices identified in past research as ethical issues:

- Cheryl Webster is an account manager in a small advertising agency. One of her largest clients, a local car dealership, plans to run a series of commercials. The client approved storyboards and the ads went to production. In casting actors to play salesmen for the dealership, the best available actor, Jon Li, was Chinese. While Webster herself didn't have anything against Asians, she was afraid that her client would dislike the ad. Webster has heard her client make racial jokes. Webster worried that she might lose the account. When Li asked Webster if he could have the job, Webster said she had already hired somebody else. Webster really had not hired anybody, because she could not find anybody who was a good actor besides Li. What should Webster have done? Hired Li or not?
- Chris Stevens is the owner of a small advertising agency. Until now, his company has worked on relatively small, regional accounts but the quality of work has attracted some national attention. Recently, Stevens was invited by a leading, national beer distributor to pitch a $150 million beer account. He has said in the past that most alcohol advertising is irresponsible in the way it targets younger adults and promotes "partying." Still, he recognizes that landing an account like this could mean great things for his agency. Stevens asks several of his employees, friends, and colleagues what to do and receives mixed answers. Some say they would have no problem working on a beer account, while others say they would be uncomfortable promoting alcohol. Stevens wonders in which

118 CHAPTER 8

direction he should take his agency. What should Stevens do? Pitch the account or decline it?

In addition to the moral dilemmas, participants were asked demographic and employment information.

The survey was posted on the Internet and respondents were recruited through the snowballing of industry contacts. The URL and a request for participation also was posted to an advertising industry listserv. Finally, 15 surveys were mailed to industry contacts in New York City. Once data collection was completed, IP addresses were used to identify and eliminate possible duplicate responses. A total of 65 completed surveys were collected. Some respondents appear to have started the survey more than once before actually completing. Of the 80 attempted responses to the Internet survey, 27.5% (22) were eliminated for this reason. Another 8 (10%) were eliminated due to nonresponse error.

WHO THE RESPONDENTS WERE AND WHAT THEY SAID

Demographically, the advertising practitioners who responded to the survey resembled the journalists who took part in the DIT. The mean age of advertising respondents was 39 years. The majority (52.4%) were female and more than 90% had college degrees, with 23.6% holding graduate degrees. These findings for age and education seem to match other industry profiles. A recent industry survey conducted by *Advertising Age* (2003) reported that men hold 51% of positions in advertising. The size of the agency in which the respondents worked ranged from small, one to three-person shops to large, international firms. More than half (54%) had worked in advertising for 10 years or less, whereas 25.4% had more than 20 years of agency experience. In sum, the respondents were well educated and were not professional novices. Because moral development is linked to educational attainment, it could be expected that advertising practitioners would score well on the DIT, as did their journalistic colleagues, and at least as well on the advertising-specific scenarios, a test of some domain expertise.

Such was not the case.

The study found that advertising professionals demonstrated considerably lower ethical reasoning than do journalists. The mean P score of advertising professionals in this sample was 31.64 ($SD = 12.1$), whereas the mean P score of journalists was 48.68 ($SD = 12.65$). In fact, the advertising professionals' mean ethical reasoning scores fall below those of most other tested professions; rather, they are in line with high school students, whose mean P score is 31, and below U.S. adults in general (P score $= 40$). However, as Table 8.1 indicates, advertising professionals' P scores were closely aligned with those generated by professionals from the business community.

Even more alarming, the advertising practitioners who responded scored even lower in ethical reasoning when asked to deliberate on advertising-specific dilemmas. The mean P score for the two advertising dilemmas was 22.7 ($SD = 14.5$), and the difference between the mean P score for the advertising dilemmas and the original DIT dilemmas was significant ($t = 5.01$, $df = 64$, $p < .001$). In other words, advertising practitioners scored significantly higher when the dilemmas were not about advertising.

These findings suggest that advertising practitioners are capable of reasoning at a higher stage of moral development, but when asked to do so in a professional setting they suspend moral judgment to focus on the financial implications of their decisions, specifically the financial implications for themselves and the client. Such reasoning clearly parallels short-term, act-based utilitarianism—a finding that is consistent with the scholarly literature on the subject.

This line of reasoning was particularly evident in the hiring scenario, specifically whether an account manager should hire an Asian actor for a car dealership commercial. When asked to rank which statement would be most important in reaching their decision, 27.7% of respondents ranked "Does the account manager have the right to make her own business decisions?" as most im-

TABLE 8.1

Mean *P* Scores of Various Professions

Seminarians/philosophers	65.1
Medical students	50.2
Practicing physicians	49.2
Journalists	48.68
Dental students	7.6
Nurses	46.3
Graduate students	44.9
Undergraduate students	43.2
Veterinary students	42.2
Navy enlisted personnel	41.6
Orthopedic surgeons	41
Adults in general	41
Business professionals	38.13
Accounting undergraduates	34.8
Accounting auditors	32.5
Advertising professionals	**31.64**
Business undergraduates	31.35
High school students	31
Prison inmates	23.7
Junior high students	20

portant. Another 27.7% ranked "Whether hiring the actor or paying attention to her client's wishes would be best for her agency's business" as most important. These statements represent schemas for personal interest moral reasoning on the DIT, the lowest level of moral development. Another 23.1% of respondents ranked the statement "Whether there is a law that forbids racial discrimination in hiring for jobs" as most important. This statement fell into the maintaining social norms schema—the second and most common level of moral development. The only other statement to rank within the top four was "Whether hiring capable men like Li would benefit society by reducing stereotypes." This stage (normative ideals and universal principles on Kohlberg's scale of response) was ranked third by 16.4% and fourth by 17.5% of respondents. None of the respondents ranked this statement as most important.

The sum of these reasons meant that nearly half, 43.1%, of respondents said they would not hire the actor, whereas 24.6% could not decide. Only 32.3% would hire him. It is important to note that the DIT privileges the reasons for making ethical choices rather than the final choices in evaluating moral development. Nonetheless, with most of the participants giving reasons that ranked relatively low on the moral development scale, it is difficult to conclude that these final choices represent deeply reflective moral thinking. This is particularly troubling because academic research has shown that racial minorities comprise an increasingly large group of consumers, whom it would be in the advertising practitioners' financial best interest to reach. In this case, a decision that privileges universal ethical principles could also have had a beneficial financial impact, something that does not always happen in advertising. Yet, participants did not appear to make that connection.

At first glance, the dilemma dealing with alcohol advertising offers some indication that advertisers look beyond profit-and-loss statements in making difficult decisions. For this scenario, 40% of respondents ranked the statement "Whether Stevens has an opportunity to produce socially responsible alcohol advertising" as most important. Ranking second most important among 15.4% of respondents was the normative/ideal schema statement "The public has a right to receive product information in order to make informed consumer choices." Another 15.6% rated this statement as third most important and 16.1% rated it fourth.

Although the ranking of these statements is encouraging, it may also be misleading insofar as they support the business decision advocated by 70.8% of respondents and leading to the greatest financial gain for themselves and their agency: pitching the account. Less than a quarter, 21.5%, of respondents said they would not pitch the alcohol account. Other statements, both representing personal interest schemas, also ranked in the top four reasons given by the participants: "Landing a major account like this will help Stevens' agency's reputation for producing big-budget, national advertising" and "A chance to work on an account like this may not come along again." The high ranking of these statements by the participants—a preponderance of personal interest schema statements—demonstrates the focus of thinking centered on financial and personal gain rather than social, and perhaps more universal, issues.

Advertising practitioners do have some company in this focus. Thorne (2000) examined the prescriptive and deliberative reasoning abilities of accountants. Prescriptive moral reasoning is defined as "the consideration of what should ideally be done to resolve a particular ethical dilemma" (Thorne, 2000, p. 141). Deliberative moral reasoning is "the formulation of an intention to act on a particular ethical dilemma" (Thorne, 2000, p. 141). Based on this dichotomy, Thorne developed two versions of the DIT. One asked respondents to answer as if they were members of a professional disciplinary committee and were, therefore, prescribing what ideally ought to occur. The other version asked respondents to answer based on what they thought realistically would occur. Thorne concluded, "It may be inferred from these results that accountants respond to social factors when formulating their ideal professional judgment and respond to self-interest in the exercise of professional judgment" (Thorne, 2000, p. 141).

However, one element of this study with advertising practitioners becomes particularly disturbing when reviewed in light of Thorne's work. The wording of the advertising-specific dilemmas asked respondents to offer prescriptive reasoning. They were asked, "What should Webster and Stevens do?" If the results among accountants are any indication, it seems likely that actual moral reasoning among advertising professionals might be even lower than the scores reported here.

There was other discouraging news. Studies have shown that ethics courses, and more specifically education, help to increase salience of moral issues for students. However, education does not take place only in the classroom. Indeed, there are many studies, particularly of journalists, that indicate that work experience—what is called *newsroom socialization*—has a profound effect on professional growth. This effect was evident with the journalists who responded to the DIT; those who had worked as investigative reporters and/or civic journalists were better ethical thinkers. Working had taught them something important.

Given this, one might expect that real-world experience might boost advertising practitioners' moral reasoning ability. But, again, such was not the case. Findings show that having worked longer in the advertising industry negatively correlated with moral reasoning ($r = -.263, p < .05$). Chronological age had no effect, a finding that is consistent with the larger literature surrounding the DIT and moral development in general. In fact, time spent in the industry was the only variable to significantly correlate with moral reasoning ability.

At this point, it is important to add a methodological caveat. Unlike the DIT survey of journalists, this survey was administered via the Web. There was no in-person interaction with the researchers. This methodological approach is quite distinct from most of the rest of the work that has been done using the DIT. It is impossible to know whether researchers who arrive in person at a workplace somehow cue participants that the study is important and needs to be taken seriously. Because the survey was taken on the Web, it is also difficult to know how much time each respondent devoted to completing it. The in-person surveys required anywhere from 25 to 60 minutes of participant time. If things were done more quickly on the Web, it is possible that the quality of moral reasoning also declined.

Although these caveats are important—and certainly cry out for additional research—this does not mean that these results should be either discarded or completely discounted. In many ways, they are consistent with the results of the DIT administered to those whose professional focus is business. However, their import remains troubling, particularly for an industry that continues to sustain heavy criticism and for professionals who are searching for ways to improve performance.

WHAT DOES THIS MEAN FOR THE INDUSTRY?

Past research has catalogued the types of ethical dilemmas faced in advertising and tried to identify the methods and standards advertisers might use to process such issues. Previous research also has offered philosophical justifications for and criticisms of advertising as an industry. Yet, until now, no one had examined why advertising appears so problematic, particularly whether advertising professionals simply lack the ability to improve the ethicality of the industry through better moral reasoning. This study is the first to provide insight into the moral reasoning abilities of advertising professionals. Unfortunately, the findings only support the many criticisms of the industry. This study indicates that advertising professionals do lack ethics, or at the very least choose not to exercise the ethical reasoning abilities they have. Additional research is now needed to understand why, and whether lack of moral reasoning translates into immoral behavior.

Research conducted in the field of accounting shows that advertisers are not alone, and offers some suggestions for further research. Studies conducted by Ponemon (1992; 1993) found that P scores of accounting professionals negatively correlate with rank. Assuming that one achieves higher rank the longer one is in the business, these findings support those indicating that advertising professionals with more experience have lower P scores.

But what does this mean for actual behavior? The accounting research indicates that the link between thinking and behavior is complex; things are not always what they seem. Ponemon (1993) conducted an experiment observing accounting students' ethical behavior. Students were told that, because of university budget cuts, they would have to pay for course handouts. They also were led to believe there would be no way to know who had actually paid; therefore, they would have the opportunity to "free ride" on other students. Ponemon found that those students with lower P scores were more likely to free ride. Interestingly, so were those students with higher P scores.

In a replication of Ponemon's study, Bay and Greenberg (2001) achieved similar results. They employed Rest et al.'s (1999) Four Component Model for an explanation. Rest's model outlines four processes that result in or give rise to moral behavior. Moral sensitivity is the ability to recognize that a situation presents a moral dilemma. Moral judgment involves the considerations that are involved in making a decision as to the correct action. The DIT measures the ability to formulate moral judgments. Moral motivation involves the weighing of moral considerations with other considerations and determining one's commitment to acting morally. Finally, moral character is having the courage to act on one's moral convictions.

Bay and Greenberg concluded that the unethical behavior found in their study occurred either because the moral judgment of the participants was not based, as the DIT is, on justice principles, or because moral judgments are "not being translated into ethical intentions because of some self-serving considerations" (Bay & Greenberg, 2001, p. 376). Focusing on the latter explanation, they suggested that unethical behavior may occur among those with high moral reasoning abilities because these people "become more cognitive in their approach to decision making and, thus, do not have the necessary emotional connection to others that may be affected" (Bay & Greenberg, 2001, p. 377). Those with lower P scores act unethically because their moral reasoning is simply more self-centered.

The low P scores among advertising professionals suggest that those in the industry would fall in this second category; they simply fail to think about larger societal issues. Yet, their replies to an open-ended question on the survey, asking "What is the biggest ethical problem facing the industry today?" showed that they are at least aware of some common criticisms of advertising and consider them to be important problems. The most common response to this question related to truth in advertising—an ethical issue that was not tested in this study. Responses included:

Honesty and responsibility in dissemination of information.

To make sure the consumer gets accurate and prompt information so he/she can make the best decision possible for him/herself.

Practicing what you preach—making good on your promises. Delivering what you advertise.

Making the commercials as honest as possible, don't try to sell something that doesn't work.

Additional research in advertising is needed to better understand how moral reasoning translates to moral intentions and behavior. It appears that advertising professionals, although they can identify important issues, may not feel motivated to reason or to act ethically. In fact, some responses to the open-ended question proved to be very thoughtful and demonstrated a clear appreciation of broad social impacts. Among those comments were:

Truthfulness, and projecting an unreal view of society to promote sales and image.

They blur the difference between wants and needs. Especially to those who can't tell the difference. The target is convinced to overextend themselves for image and status.

The perpetuation of the image of a "stupid" America. One that—when viewed through the way we advertise to ourselves—finds us all to be shallow, vain, uninformed, undereducated, etc.

Even so, the lack of moral reasoning is even more pronounced when faced with an industry-specific dilemma. The findings of this study suggest that, as with other business professions, the problem rests in the balancing of often contradictory professional and societal values. The questions for future research are why do advertisers choose to suspend moral judgment and how might they be motivated to do the right thing?

Part III

IMPLICATIONS FOR TEACHERS, SCHOLARS, AND PROFESSIONALS

CHAPTER 9

Teaching Journalists About Ethics: What This Study Suggests

IS IT FUTILE?

A consistent and potentially discouraging finding in the multiple studies that represent this research is that when asked directly participants said that their university-level training in ethics made no difference in how they thought about professional problems. Instead, they focused on the importance of professional socialization. The statistical analyses support this conclusion.

Although it is important to acknowledge these findings, we also believe a deeper reading of the data, coupled with our own professional experience as journalists, suggest a more sanguine interpretation. Ethical journalists were those professionals who had a strong internal sense of the appropriate professional choices. In many instances, that strong internal sense had to act as counterweight to a professional environment—the same environmental that journalists credited with influencing their decisions. What should readers and journalism students make of these two claims?

First, we have no doubt that in this study of journalists, as in many others beginning with the seminal study "Newsroom Socialization" (Breed, 1955) and continuing through work such as *Custodians of Conscience* (Ettema & Glasser, 1998), the workplace clearly establishes norms and, at its best, promotes ethical discussion. When working journalists say that their professional environment influences them, there is substantial empirical evidence to support this claim. What is less clear is the mental mechanism that journalists and advertising practitioners bring to evaluate the ethical import of what goes on in the workplace. Yet, it is clear—again from scholarly studies, such as *Good Work* (Gardner et al., 2001)—that professionals are engaged in such an evaluation.

Although there are certainly many influences, we suggest that an examination of the journalists' own recounting of why they made the decisions they did reveals influences that extend beyond the newsroom and into the classroom. Newsrooms seldom offer seminars on the role of law in reporting or advertising; professional organizations may provide "brush up" sessions, but our participants attended relatively few such meetings. It seems reasonable to suggest that much of what the journalists and advertising practitioners in our studies knew about the law—and the First Amendment—came from their classroom training.

Both the professionals who took the DIT and the IRE members who responded to the survey discussed privacy, deception, and truth. These issues certainly arise in the workplace (as well as in private life), but it is clear from the responses that workplace encounters with the issues could not completely account for both the depth of thought and the language used to convey it. Here, too, we saw subtle influences from outside the newsroom—everything from the moral imagination to a particular set of facts that raised a certain ethical question to the way that many journalists balanced competing duties. It is impossible to completely catalogue these influences. However, along with mom and dad and everyday life, we'd like to the suggest that the classroom and ethics instruction are not as absent as our self-reporting participants might like to believe.

We'd also suggest that the responses to our questions do not indicate that there is a profound disconnect between the classroom and the newsroom when it comes to ethics, as some recent work has indicated (Hansen, 2002). The students who participated in the experiments, and the professionals who took the DIT, were more similar than they were different—at least when it came to recognizing and reconciling ethical choices.

Perhaps the more significant disjuncture is between what journalists believe is important, even though it raises ethical concerns, and what the public is willing to tolerate (Riffe et al., 2003). Although the nature of the disconnection between journalists and their many audiences is sometimes troubling, to journalists among others, it is cavalier to suggest that long-term professionals make choices only to conform to a newsroom or capitalistic ethos. None of the most recent scholarship on journalists suggests that this is the case, and we believe the weight of the data presented in this book supports that stream of findings. Discussing professional roles and duties is not a topic of newsroom conversation. Yet, it is evident that thinking about these issues drives ethical thinking, even in the face of public misunderstanding and disapproval. Thinking about these issues has its origins in the classroom.

Instead, we would like to suggest that it is education, and professional training that includes discussion of ethics, that is responsible for a general outlook as well as specific ways of thinking through difficult dilemmas. Asserting that professional education matters, despite self-report that it does not, also parallels one of the most robust findings in research on moral development: The more education one has, in general, the better one's ethical thinking will become. Acknowledged or not, teachers of media ethics at the university level are playing an important role in the future of the profession.

BUT WHAT SHOULD BE TAUGHT?

Participants in the studies reported here also provide some important guidance about the issues that classroom ethicists need to continue—or begin— to address. We believe the findings highlight the following.

The Need to Develop and Expand the Ethical Underpinnings of the Law, Particularly the Law of Mass Communication.   Legal scholars have suggested for decades that it is important for many professionals to understand how philosophy "fills" the law with concepts and ways of thinking that are ethically potent. Often, and for sound reasons, courses in mass media law emphasize the learning of precedent. This is important, and in a professional world it is essential if journalists are to understand the legal issues facing them on questions such as libel and information ownership. However, if professional thinking about ethics includes an element of "touching base" with the law—as it did for many participants in these studies—then it is important that such a base be filled with philosophy as well as a specific legal history. Few university-level courses in media ethics devote much attention to an ethical analysis of the law. Yet, it is clear from these data that professionals would use such a touchstone.

The Need to Breathe New Life Into Normative Theory—the Institutional Role of the Media—and Connect That Theory to Individual Acts. Institutions are difficult territory, whether your academic home is philosophy or journalism. However, the emerging work in professional ethics generally—and mass communication specifically—suggests that institutional analysis and theory lags behind daily decision making, whether that decision is about managed care or agenda setting. Communitarian scholars have begun this effort, but working professionals need both intellectual and practical tools to take advantage of it. How can classroom efforts help jour-

nalists build communities that can withstand both the pressures of professional competition and government and corporate demands—without
requiring what philosophers would call *supererogatory acts*, such as whistle-
blowing that costs a career or becoming the irritating newsroom gadfly and
conscience? Building a community of heroes is not a purely academic exercise in the current environment; working journalists need to meet institutional mass with a power and intellectual force of their own.

***Renew the Emphasis on Social Justice, Grounded not Just in a
Philosophical Conception but in a Political One.*** If there is a way to
begin to undo the long-term legacy of racial intolerance and stereotyping
that lingers in U.S. culture and that we found evident in decisions that both
journalists and advertising practitioners made, then an emphasis on recognizing and understanding the weaker party would seem to be an important
step forward. So too would a professional standard of excellence that places
justice on a more equal footing with truth. The journalists who took the
DIT clearly balanced competing claims, and the fact that their logic did not
leave them with monolithic results is commendable. Additionally, the fact
that they could not consciously recognize and articulate the relationship
among all the stakeholders should, it would seem, be amenable to education. Perhaps a classroom approach of digitally manipulating every photo
in editing and reporting classes so that skin tone, and hence race, could be
foregrounded as part of a discussion would be a good tool. Discussions
about the appropriateness of doing bad things to bad people—in a professional sense—and acknowledging that impulse and its problems also would
help. However, in a profession with a society-wide role, renewed emphasis
on social justice in conjunction with classical ethical theory would seem essential at this juncture. Furthermore, there is some indication that in the
professional world, such work happens. Samantha Power's Pulitzer
Prize-winning book *The Problem from Hell* (2002) is but one example of self-
aware journalism that places justice at the forefront of reporting.

***Concomitant With an Emphasis on Social Justice Should Be More
Discussion of the "Ethics of Care."*** This suggestion is particularly
problematic for a generation of faculty facing a generation of students who
are both eager to please (the faculty) and reluctant to confront (their story
subjects). If there is such a thing as assertive care—and our experience as
both professionals and parents would indicate that there might be—then
ethics instructors need to operationalize it in the classroom and teach it to
their students. Journalists cannot operate as milquetoasts, but neither can

they fulfill their obligations as bulldozers. An intellectually focused middle ground, in an Aristotelian sense, is what is in order. The reasons for caring, and the reasons for getting tough—and the connection between the two—need to be explored and fleshed out. This will not make decisions, such as the ones explored in the "junkie kids" case, less difficult, but it may allow professionals to understand that thinking through such cases represents a consistent stream of reasoning about professional role in a robust democracy. Such an understanding is particularly important for young journalists as they begin their careers and enter the world of newsroom pressure and socialization.

AND WHY DOES IT MATTER?

Early scholarship, indeed some myths, have tended to portray journalists as lone, creative inquisitors, unencumbered by corporate ties or much education, a meager challenge to the powers that be. In some instances, this myth remains true, but the daily reality is now different.

Journalists are well educated; the vast majority of the participants in these studies had earned a bachelors degree and a sizable minority had obtained some graduate education. This level of educational attainment is true for the students who took part in the experiments as well.

Journalists work for corporations, some of them monstrously large. They are encumbered—and enabled—by a professional history that includes successfully challenging the powerful, as well as failing in such efforts. They are visible, upper middle class, and are considered important—important enough to criticize and despise as well as praise—by the majority of Americans. As this study demonstrated, they possess some domain expertise. They are members of the power elite, and the institutions they represent are among the most powerful on the globe.

These are morally relevant professional facts. Journalists are not powerful in every situation, nor in every story. But they are in many, as are the corporations that pay them. Teaching journalism ethics—just like the ethics instruction in law or in medicine—needs to accept that journalists, like lawyers and doctors, enter into the ethics arena as powerful, or potentially powerful, actors.

It is individual and institutional power, more than any other single "fact" of professional life, that argues for ethics instruction. Furthermore, if journalists themselves are to be understood in their own words as reviewed in the foregoing chapters, such instruction will fall on fertile—if crowded—ground. Although the last chapter in this book explores the ways that academic psychology and philosophy can support such teaching, these studies make clear that there is a need for such instruction and that it can make a difference. Moral development in a professional setting is most significant only as it becomes reflected in professional performance at large. Understanding how journalists think about ethical issues is key to elevating first the discussion, then the understanding, and finally—with some help—professional practice.

CHAPTER 10

Theory: A Moving Target

INTERDISCIPLINARY WORK: THINKING THROUGH
IMPLICATIONS AT THE DISCIPLINE'S EDGE

Since its inception, moral development theory has had multidisciplinary implications. Although originally developed by psychologists, the nature of the subject matter—moral thinking—had implications beyond psychology. Indeed, Piaget's work, beginning as it did between the two World Wars, became most influential after World War II when academics as well as politicians tried figure out at the deepest, human level what had happened in Nazi Germany.

This book, too, comes at a particular time in history, one when social institutions are under serious and long-term stress, and where many of the social sciences, psychology among them, are integrating both the knowledge and the tools of sciences, such as biology, to further disciplinary understanding. The fact that many disciplines speak to one question is a potential pitfall; saying something uninformed in a biological or philosophical sense will encourage scholars in those disciplines to reject essential findings. The opportunity to enrich theory is equally great. Psychology, professional ethics, and philosophy have much to say to one another. This chapter represents our attempt to develop interdisciplinary insights, always keeping in mind that theoretical development is possible only when disciplinary understandings are taken seriously.

THE IMPLICATIONS OF VISUALS:
A NEW TOOL FOR MORAL THINKING

Moral development theory has always been an effort to explain and synthesize a lived experience. Piaget began this effort with a children's game that was based in geometry and visual information in addition to words. The boys whom Piaget studied learned to render ethical thought into concrete decisions that could be expressed visually as well as verbally. Kohlberg's work was exclusively word based, although those words reflected a larger lived experience. The word-based approach has dominated scholarly research for more than the past 3 decades, but we suggest that visual thinking, whether called to mind by a Kohlberg-like narrative or the lived experience of the women Gilligan studied, has always been implied.

One of the central and important findings of this book was that visual information influences moral reasoning. For the professional journalists who took the DIT, a picture appears to have stimulated the moral imagination, at least as far as stakeholders were concerned. In these instances, thinking about stakeholders improved moral reasoning. Philosophers have long suggested that ethical thinking that foregrounds stakeholders—whether in the form of Rawls' veil of ignorance or Ross' multiple duties—should promote good-quality ethical reasoning. Both the statistical and qualitative results of this study confirm this insight. Philosophers may respond with "ho-hum, of course we knew this," but demonstrating the effect of such an understanding on concrete ethical choices moves the debate ahead.

However, pictures did not always carry the kind of information that improved ethical reasoning. When images conveyed information about race, the central route processing that seems to have dominated the ethical thinking of the participants who took the DIT sometimes appeared overwhelmed by previous, stereotypical understandings. This appeared to have crowded out—perhaps by literally influencing the pathways through the brain that such information traveled—deeper reflection by those who participated in the experiments. The stakeholders became something "other"—a mental construct that was culturally loaded in a way that diminished rather than enhanced the moral imagination. If the current disciplinary understanding of psychology is both accepted and taken seriously, then the fact that this kind of content in visual images seemed to influence how they are processed and acted on carries theoretical weight. Content and context should influence moral thinking. Visual information adds to both. The key will be to attempt to determine how to employ visual information that encourages central route processing rather than a more peripheral route.

The findings about race are reinforced in a different way by advertising practitioners. Even though visual information was not involved in the advertising scenario, those who participated certainly needed to visualize the ad. The fact that moral thinking by advertising practitioners was dictated in many instances by the racist views of a client only suggest that the issue of race remains a difficult problem for the industry, even after the larger American culture has struggled to change.

Thomas Jefferson once called slavery America's peculiar institution. We suggest that race could be characterized in the same way. Although our findings about race are discouraging, they also provide both academic psychologists and media professionals with a different way of thinking about the issue. In the United States, race has had a visual information component—one that historically appears to have overwhelmed the country's best political and ethical thinking. Understanding that visual information, because it can be processed in different ways in the brain, may have differential effects, depending on the content of the visuals themselves, and may provide one mechanism to begin to undo the stereotypical and peripheral response and substitute a more central route approach. How to do that is obviously a topic for further academic research and for professional training—one that arms potential professionals with the arguments and insights that summon higher-level reasoning. However, we would not like these findings on race to obscure the larger point: Visual information appeared to promote higher levels of moral reasoning. Further studies of moral development—as well as understanding professional performance—can make use of this finding.

THE IMPLICATIONS FOR PROFESSIONAL JOURNALISTS: MORAL THINKING HAPPENS

In a time when the profession itself is under internal and external stress, it can't be said often enough: This study demonstrates that journalists are both good and subtle moral thinkers. The members of Investigative Reporters and Editors demonstrated that they understood both the obvious and subtle implications of deception. Furthermore, they were willing to engage in fine-grained thinking about the issue. Their thinking reflects the larger universal principles of the profession: Deceiving your audience is almost always unacceptable (unless you clearly do so to save lives, as in the case of troop movements and national security). Omitting information, in a profession whose central societal role is providing information, is less morally culpable than is making affirmative statements that are outright deceptive. Lying to liars can sometimes—but only sometimes—be justified, and journalists, just as philosophers who have written about the topic, are sometimes uneasy with the ethical compromise that this particular decision represents.

The journalists who took the DIT reasoned dynamically. The participants who thought about ethics in this book did so at levels that reflected both universal understandings as well as more conventional reasoning. They balanced privacy and truth, the needs and wishes of a wide range of stakeholders—from society at large to individuals who became concrete to them in the process of their thinking. They were mindful that, in a society based in law, legal decisions could and probably should have an impact on what they would write or broadcast. Sometimes, like many other adults, they relied on the law more exclusively than deeper and more philosophically based reasoning could support. But many who considered the law also considered moral principles, including those that the law represents as well as those the law only incompletely codifies.

Just as the authors of *Good Work* found, the journalists in these studies thought well about their profession, not only in the sense of the quality of their reasoning but also in the sense of expectations and aspirations. Journalism and news reporting performed an important public service for many of the participants, and they pegged their ethical thinking to a standard that, at its most fundamental, had a universal quality to it. Knowledge about journalism, as a set of practices and as an institution that performs an essential societal role, provided a significant and measurable level of domain expertise for the journalists who participated in these studies. To the best of our knowledge, this empirical evidence of domain expertise is also a significant finding. It adds evidence to the scholarly debate over whether journalists and journalism should be considered a profession or a craft—an issue that is of interest to philosophers, particularly those who study applied ethics, as well as to practitioners. These findings suggest that there is more to being a journalist than learning to write in inverted pyramid style and mastering nonlinear editing. Thinking like a journalist involves moral reflection, done both dynamically and at a level that in most instances equals or exceeds that of members of the other learned professions.

This is not to say that the system itself does not provide considerable stress, as well as one of the major contradictions in these findings. In one study, analysis of the responses of the journalists who took the DIT suggested that internal influences—not a competitive environment or the type of medium—were most important in ethical thinking. Members of Investigative Reporters and Editors suggested otherwise. They noted that competition placed pressure on moral thinking, and that television, with its demands for visual information, placed a different emphasis on what philosophers call the "morally relevant facts."

We believe the weight of the evidence in this book and others that have examined these issues suggests that competition can have a significant effect on moral reasoning. There is much anecdotal evidence to indicate that competition is both influential and, in general, deleterious. The journalists whose thinking is examined in this book suggested that they knew competition was a problem, that they exerted strong efforts to make sound choices within a competitive environment, and that despite these efforts, they believed it was occasionally too influential. This does not mean that the journalists who said competition was a significant factor in their decision making were any the less influenced and motivated by the internal factors that appeared to predominate in the thinking of the journalists who took the DIT. Rather, it suggests that reporters work in an environment that expressed itself in different ways. Some stories simply are not competitive; others are. Good ethical thinking should allow a professional to consider both elements and to make different decisions based on this context.

It is important to note here that other studies, using different methods and asking slightly different questions, have uncovered much the same kind of reasoning. The journalists who participated in the interviews that became the core of *Good Work* maintained both high professional ideals and the practical knowledge that the economic nature of journalism-as-business represented a corrosive element within the profession. The authors of *Good Work* characterized these seemingly conflicting understandings as evidence of a profession that is "out of alignment" with some of its more basic understandings. Rather than focusing on the internal cross-signals, the authors suggested that the contradiction itself represented the opportunity for significant professional growth in both an individual and institutional sense. We are equally optimistic. The fact that journalists acknowledge that their environment presents real constraints can help the profession hone its own moral sensibility. As Kohlberg noted, moving up the stages of moral development often occurs when the conflicts in one stage can be resolved only by a change in thinking. In an institutional sense, journalism as a profession appears to be at the same nexus, one that has potential for development as well as less happy consequences.

However, the questions that the influence of medium and competition raise also promote important theoretical questions. Central among these, we believe, is the impact of speed, particularly when human beings have to select, either consciously or out of habit, a central or peripheral processing route. It is important to note that in this book, as well as in the accounts of other scholars, speed has never been a central issue for the participants. In this book, we gave the participants as much time as they were willing to take to complete both the DIT and the experiments. The same can be said for the students whom Kohlberg interviewed (most of those interviews took 30 to 60 minutes) and the women whom Gilligan studied. Intuitively, most human beings understand that more time can sometimes produce more reflection and better thinking. However, psychologists note that peripheral, stereotypical processing is, among other things, a mental energy saver. Additionally, philosophers suggest that ethical habits—the practice of thinking through and making decisions over and over again—contributes not only to character but also to solid moral responses under pressure. Again, to our knowledge, no one has ever empirically studied what happens to ethical thinking when time for thought is rationed.

Yet, time for thinking is one of the environmental factors that is changing journalism. Whether it is the 24-hour cable news cycle, the Web presence of most print media, or the international and satellite-connected nature of most broadcast news, journalists do not have as much time to think as they once did. Professional experience may mitigate these developments to some degree, and the journalists who took part in these studies were not novices. However, professional experience may not be able to completely counter what psychologists are beginning to understand about how the brain works—on moral questions and on many others. Given the findings about the influence of visual images on moral thinking, it would seem important to investigate whether time restrictions on decision making would have any effect on the quality of thought and the level of moral development that appears to be reflected in responses to the DIT. Journalists are certainly not the only professionals who have to make very timely choices. Patients would die if surgeons did not act quickly, and both attorneys and the clergy often have to render advice when timing is almost everything. However, studying the influence of time constraints on ethical reasoning has, to the best of our knowledge, yet to be studied in a systematic, empirical way. Such an effort would clearly have implications for many professions, and perhaps provide additional insights into information processing as well.

Second, certain sorts of ethical issues were the focus of this study—primarily those that are part of the newsgathering process and focus on the decisions that individual journalists and their editors make. In many ways, the issues studied in this book also reflect the larger field of moral development and philosophy; we have privileged the morally autonomous actor. In this book, we have focused on issues of deception, truth telling, privacy, and the institutional and political role of the media. However, as the work with advertising practitioners suggests, in the professional world individuals often work within a system or an institution.

Ethical questions that function on the systemic or institutional level were not part of this study, but they are part of professional life. As philosopher John M. Doris noted, "More generally, I've no reason to deny that some regimes may be more conducive to moral decency than others" (Doris, 2002, p. 125). Advertisers have to respond to a client; physicians have to respond to a system of managed care. These institutional constraints are only incompletely acknowledged in this work, but as the answers from advertising professionals indicate, institutional constraints can make a profound difference in decision making. This acknowledgment has real practical significance, because certainly it is relatively more difficult to picture economic survival of a newspaper or a job than it is to picture a person whose privacy might be invaded. Both are legitimate stakeholders, but one appears more accessible to at least some form of representation. Different levels of abstraction and thinking may be required to tackle institutional questions of ethics, and this study provides little insight into what, if any, differences might surface in a systematic investigation.

Finally, it is very important that readers of this book understand that this work was done in a very American context—not only of the media system but of some cultural understandings (race, the First Amendment) as well. Moral development scholars have long acknowledged that most of their work is based on data collected in the United States and analyzed in that context. What the context of a different culture, and a different media system, might produce are important theoretical questions. For journalists, they have practical import as well, because the U.S. news media dominate international news coverage, an institutional structure that is unlikely to change in the immediate future. Here, we can suggest only further research, fueled by the understanding that although the hard-wired human brain varies relatively little with cultural shifts, how elements are perceived and analyzed might be profoundly influenced by culture. Taking studies of moral development to other, non-U.S. cultures could provide important insights about the relative importance of external compared to internal motivations and what becomes included in central compared to peripheral pathways.

THE IMPLICATIONS FOR PHILOSOPHY: MULTIPLE UNIVERSAL PRINCIPLES AND DIFFERENTIAL MORAL WEIGHT

Philosophers have long asserted that psychology is not philosophy. However, that does not mean that the two disciplines do not have some important things to say to one another.

First, it is important for moral development theory to more richly incorporate multiple universal principles in its framework than is currently the case. Moral development theory, particularly the work of Kohlberg on which the DIT is based, focuses on justice and rights. These are important ethical concerns, but they are not exhaustive. Our analysis of the participants' responses to the DIT suggests that issues of connection, the contribution of Gilligan specifically, and feminist philosophy are just as important. For thinking about moral development to progress, instruments that measure development need to incorporate a greater body of universal understandings and to move equally from the rights-based tradition to the ethics of care. In this, we believe that our participants are actually ahead of the theory, because many of them demonstrated an ability to reason in this way, particularly when allowed to express their thoughts in their own words. Although is it almost certainly unfair to ask that ethicists develop the philosophical equivalent of the universal field theory in physics, it is not too much to hope that current work would seek some integration of universal principles for both conceptual and practical application.

Second, we believe that philosophy could profit from a serious reconsideration of the importance of stakeholders on ethical decision making. Whether it is the work of Rawls (1971) or Habermas (1989), philosophy as a field has made some assumptions about the nature of stakeholders and their relative significance in ethical reasoning. The results of the studies in this book challenge some of those assumptions. Take Rawls' veil of ignorance (1971), which asserts that, behind the veil everyone is equal both in social and political status and in standing. Under such conditions, Rawls postulated, everyone would agree to act in such a way as to maximize individual liberty and to protect the weaker party when all parties emerge from behind the veil. But what happens when some stakeholders are more equal than others—and likely to remain so? This same problem is what rendered Habermas' (1989) conceptualization of the public sphere a worthy theoretical insight that favors process over outcome. However, in professional practice, whether it is law, medicine, or journalism, outcomes matter. This is the problem: stakeholders of unequal moral weight, facing advertising practitioners. If professionals—and even academic philosophers—are unwilling to condemn entire enterprises such as persuasion as unethical, then thoughtful solutions to the advertising–stakeholder dilemma need to be a focus of philosophical inquiry.

Third, we find ourselves very much in agreement with the general thesis of John. M. Doris who, in one short volume, tested philosophical notions of character against the findings of social psychology and found the concept of character incomplete. Doris (2002) contended that environment is crucial to ethical decision making, and cited studies from Stanley Milgram forward to buttress his contentions: "There are obvious affinities between contextualist approaches to intelligence and situationist approaches to personality. In fact, a contextualist approach to cognition helps explain situationist findings on moral behavior; if moral behavior has a strong cognitive component (broadly construed) and cognition is highly context-sensitive, one should expect moral behavior to be highly context-sensitive" (Doris, 2002, p. 70). Philosophers tend to deal with context as an abstraction. However, thinking in the field that particularizes context, particularly the kind of context that could make moral action more rather than less common, would be a contribution on many levels. Communitarian philosophers have begun some of this work, as have some feminists. However, much more remains to be done. The impact of such philosophically based exploration would be multidisciplinary, of help to psychologists and a variety of scholars who study professional ethics in its many formulations.

Appendix

PHOTO DILEMMA

Pete Stevens is one of your newspaper's best photographers. He has just returned from an area of town frequented by drug dealers and addicts. Pete has a compelling photo to go with a story on the effects of drugs on children. The photo shows two children, Maria, age 5, and her 3-year-old brother, Jorge, whose parents are addicts. The parents think their children don't see what they do, but as this photo shows, the children have playing "junkie" down to a detailed routine.

The photo was taken in a public alley, and Maria and Jorge's parents gave your photographer permission to take pictures of the children for publication. Since then, however, the children's grandmother has heard about the photo and called your newsroom to ask that you not run the photo. There are mixed opinions in the newsroom. You have the final say. What would you do?

HIDDEN CAMERAS

TV reporter Lauren Gray is investigating patient abuse by home health providers—private agencies that send health workers into homes to do everything from housecleaning to semi-skilled nursing. The Better Business Bureau has logged multiple complaints about patient abuse and so has the state nursing home board, but they lack authority to act. District Attorney Paul Johnson tells Gray that while his office has begun a criminal investigation, it has been stymied by a lack of evidence or by frail or elderly witnesses who may be unconvincing in court. Gray is urged to pursue the story, the officials involved agreeing to release public documents and go on the record.

Seven people receiving in-home care have agreed to let Gray place hidden cameras in their homes for a week so she can tape the care providers. Should wrongdoing occur, Gray plans to speak to the provider, show the tape and ask for an on-the-record response. If no wrongdoing occurs, Gray plans to report this as well. You are the executive producer who must decide whether to use the hidden cameras. What would you do?

DIT QUESTIONNAIRE

Thinking back to the problem of whether to run the photo of the children playing junkie, please rate why you made the decision you did, in terms of each of the following:

Because I'm very interested in issues like this and enjoy the challenge of presenting it in the right way.

Not at all for this reason			Somewhat		Very much for this reason	
1	2	3	4	5	6	7

Because it seemed to me like the right thing to do.

Not at all for this reason			Somewhat		Very much for this reason	
1	2	3	4	5	6	7

Because I would feel guilty, ashamed, or bad about myself, like I wasn't doing my duty, if I did/didn't run the photo.

Not at all for this reason			Somewhat		Very much for this reason	
1	2	3	4	5	6	7

Because others expected me to run/not run the photo, or because the situation demanded it.

Not at all for this reason			Somewhat		Very much for this reason	
1	2	3	4	5	6	7

Please tell us in your own words why you made the decision you did: _____
_____
_____
_____

Thinking back to the problem of whether to use hidden cameras, please rate why you made the decision you did, in terms of each of the following:

Because I'm very interested in issues like this and enjoy the challenge of presenting it in the right way.

Not at all for this reason			Somewhat		Very much for this reason	
1	2	3	4	5	6	7

Because it seemed to me like the right thing to do.

Not at all for this reason			Somewhat		Very much for this reason	
1	2	3	4	5	6	7

Because I would feel guilty, ashamed, or bad about myself, like I wasn't doing my duty, if I did/didn't use the hidden cameras.

Not at all for this reason			Somewhat		Very much for this reason	
1	2	3	4	5	6	7

Because others expected me to use/not use the hidden camera, or because the situation demanded it.

Not at all for this reason			Somewhat		Very much for this reason	
1	2	3	4	5	6	7

Please tell us in your own words why you made the decision you did: _____
_____
_____
_____

Using the following scales, please rate how important to you each of the following is when you are faced with a difficult ethical decision:

Whether our competition has the story.
Not at all important   Very important
        1   2   3   4   5   6   7

The impact of the decision on my career.
Not at all important   Very important
        1   2   3   4   5   6   7

Standards established by my employer.
Not at all important   Very important
        1   2   3   4   5   6   7

How my colleagues would handle the same story.
Not at all important   Very important
        1   2   3   4   5   6   7

What the people who are the subject of this photo or story will think when they see it.
Not at all important   Very important
        1   2   3   4   5   6   7

Ethical standards prevailing in American journalism today.
Not at all important   Very important
        1   2   3   4   5   6   7

The public's need for information and right to know
Not at all important   Very important
        1   2   3   4   5   6   7

Religion as the true basis for professional ethics.
Not at all important   Very important
        1   2   3   4   5   6   7

Legal issues such as libel and invasion of privacy.
Not at all important   Very important
        1   2   3   4   5   6   7

That my own standard of ethics are set to the level I feel is set by my employer.
Not at all important   Very important
        1   2   3   4   5   6   7

Maintaining credibility with the audience.
Not at all important   Very important
        1   2   3   4   5   6   7

My own sense of what is right and wrong.
Not at all important   Very important
        1   2   3   4   5   6   7

Advice from my organization's legal counsel.
Not at all important   Very important
  1 2 3 4 5 6 7

My personal commitment to universal ethical principles.
Not at all important   Very important
  1 2 3 4 5 6 7

The support of others on the staff.
Not at all important   Very important
  1 2 3 4 5 6 7

The teachings of my religion.
Not at all important   Very important
  1 2 3 4 5 6 7

How independent does your job allow you to be?
Not at all independent   Very independent
  1 2 3 4 5 6 7

How much say do you have over the assignments you work on?
None   A lot
  1 2 3 4 5 6 7

How much are you allowed to take part in making decisions that affect your work?.
Not much   Very much
  1 2 3 4 5 6 7

How much investigative journalism are you involved with?
None   A Lot
  1 2 3 4 5 6 7

How committed to investigative journalism would you say your news organization is?
Not very committed   Very committed
  1 2 3 4 5 6 7

How much civic or public journalism are you involved with?
None   A Lot
  1 2 3 4 5 6 7

How committed to civic or public journalism would you say your news organization is?
Not very committed   Very committed
  1 2 3 4 5 6 7

What is your job title? _____

How long (in years) have you been in journalism? _____

How many journalism awards have you won in the last 5 years? _____

Please list your awards: _____

What is the size of your news organization?
Print (greatest circulation): _____ Broadcast (Market area, DMA): _____

What area of the country are you in?
☐ Northeast ☐ South ☐ Midwest ☐ Northwest ☐ Southwest ☐ West

Please check all organizations that you belong to:
☐ Society of Professional Journalists (SPJ) ☐ Investigative Reporters and Editors (IRE)
☐ Committee of Concerned Journalists ☐ Society of News Design (SND)
☐ Radio-Television News Directors Association(RTNDA)
☐ American Society of Newspaper Editors (ASNE)
☐ News Press Photographers Association (NPPA)
☐ National Association of Black Journalists (NABJ)
☐ National Association of Hispanic Journalists (NAHJ)
☐ National Association of Asian-American Journalists (NAAAJ)
Other: _____

In the last year, how many professional seminars, conferences and workshops have you been to?
☐ None ☐ 1 or 2 ☐ 3 or 4 ☐ 5 or 6 ☐ 7 or 8 ☐ 9 or more

Education
☐ Less than high school ☐ High school graduate ☐ Some college
☐ Bachelor's degree ☐ Some graduate school ☐ Graduate degree
Other: _____

Age: _____ ☐ Male ☐ Female

What race do you consider yourself?
☐ Caucasian ☐ African American ☐ Asian ☐ Hispanic ☐ American Indian
☐ Mixed Other: _____

Generally speaking, do you think of yourself as a Republican, Democrat, Independent, or what?
Strong Democrat   Independent   Strong Republican
1   2   3   4   5   6   7
Other: _____

Where would you place your political views on this scale?
Extremely liberal   Neutral   Extremely Conservative
        1   2   3   4   5   6   7

Would you describe yourself as:
Extremely religious   Neutral   Extremely non-religious
        1   2   3   4   5   6   7

What is your religious preference?
☐ Protestant ☐ Catholic ☐ Jewish ☐ None Other: _____

Where would you place your religious beliefs on this scale?
Fundamentalist   Neutral   Liberal
        1   2   3   4   5   6   7

THANK YOU!

148

References

Abbott, V., Black, J. B., & Smith, E. E. (1985). The representation of scripts in memory. *Journal of Memory and Language, 24,* 179–199.

Advertising Age. (2003). Ad Age special report salary survey. Retrieved December 12, 2003, from www.adage.com/news.cms?newsID=39244

Allen, P. W., & Ng, C. K. (2001). Self interest among CPAs may influence their moral reasoning. *Journal of Business Ethics, 33*(1), 29–35.

Bagdikian, B. (2000). *The media monopoly* (6th ed.). Boston: Preston.

Babbie, E. (1990). *Survey research methods.* Belmont, CA: Wadsworth.

Baker, S. (1999). Five baselines for justification in persuasion. *Journal of Mass Media Ethics, 14*(2), 69–81.

Bargh, J. A. (1999). The cognitive monster: The case against the controllability of automatic stereotype effects. In S. Chaiken & Y. Trope (Eds.), *Dual-process theories in social psychology* (pp. 361–382). New York: Guilford.

Barry, A. M. (1997). *Visual intelligence: Perception, image, and manipulation in visual communication.* Albany: State University of New York Press.

Basil, M. D. (1996). The use of student samples in communication research. *Journal of Broadcasting & Electronic Media, 40,* 431–440.

Bay, D., & Greenberg, R. (2001). The relationship of the DIT and behavior: A replication. *Issues in Accounting Education, 16*(3), 367–380.

Beam, R. (1993). The impact of group ownership variables on organizational professionalism at daily newspapers. *Journalism Quarterly, 70,* 907–918.

Belenky, M. F., et al. (1986). *Women's ways of knowing.* New York: Basic Books.

Bernstein, C., & Woodward, B. (1974). *All the president's men.* New York: Simon & Schuster.

Black, J. (1985, Fall/Winter). The case against mass media codes of ethics. *Journal of Mass Media Ethics, 1*(1), 14–21.

Black, J., Barney, R. D., & Van Tubergen, G. N. (1979). Moral development and belief systems of journalists. *Mass Communication Review, 6,* 4–16.

Black, J., Steele, B., & Barney, R. (1997). *Doing ethics in journalism: A handbook with case studies.* Boston: Allyn & Bacon.

Bok, S. (1989). *Lying: Moral choice in public and private life* (2nd ed.). New York: Random House. (Original work published 1978)

Borden, S. (2000). "A model for evaluating journalists resistance to business constrains." *Journal of Mass Media Ethics, 15*(3), 149–166.

Borden, S. L. (1996). Choice processes in a newspaper ethics case. *Communication Monographs, 64*, 65–81.

Borden, S. L., & Pritchard, M. (1997). News sources and deception. In E. D. Cohen & D. Elliot (Eds.), *Journalism ethics: A handbook* (pp. 102–106). Santa Barbara, CA: ABC-CLIO.

Breed, W. (1955). Social control in the newsroom. *Social Forces, 33*, 326–335.

Brosius, H. B. (1993). The effects of emotional pictures in television news. *Communication Research, 20*, 105–124.

Buller, D. B., & Burgoon, J. K. (1996). Interpersonal deception theory. *Communication Theory, 6*(3), 203–242.

Burgoon, J. K. (1980). Nonverbal communication research in the 1970's: An overview. In D. Nimmo (Ed.), *Communication Yearbook IV* (pp. 179–197). New Brunswick, NJ: Transaction.

Catholic Church. (1996). Ethics in advertising. Retrieved March 15, 1996, from http://www.tasc.ac.uk/cc/briefing/9604002.htm

Chiricos, T., Eschholz, S., & Gertz, M. (1997). Crime, news and fear of crime: Toward an identification of audience effects. *Social Problems, 44*(3), 342–358.

Chisholm, R., & Freehan, T. (1977). The intent to deceive. *Journal of Philosophy, 74*(3), 143–159.

Christians, C. (1980). *Teaching ethics in journalism education.* Hastings-on-Hudson, NY: The Hastings Center.

Christians, C. G., Fackler, M., Rotzoll, K. B., & Brittain McKee, K. (1997). *Media ethics: Cases and moral reasoning* (5th ed.). New York: Longman.

Christians, C. G., Ferre, J. P., & Fackler, P. M. (1993). *Good news: Social ethics and the press.* New York: Oxford University Press.

Cohen, C. E. (1981). Goals and schemata in person perception: Making sense from the stream of behavior. In N. Cantor & J. F. Kihlstrom (Eds.), *Personality, cognition, and social interaction* (pp. 45–68). Hillsdale, NJ: Lawrence Erlbaum Associates.

Cook, T. D., & Campbell, D. T. (1979). *Quasi-experimentation: design and analysis issues for field settings.* Chicago: Rand-McNally.

Cooper, T. W., Clifford, G. C., Plude, F. F., & White, R. A. (1989). *Communication ethics and global change.* New York: Longman.

Courtright, J. A. (1996). Rationally thinking about nonprobability. *Journal of Broadcasting & Electronic Media, 40*, 414–421.

Crisp, R. (1987). Persuasive advertising, autonomy, and the creation of desire. *Journal of Business Ethics, 6*, 413–418.

Crockett, W. H. (1988). Schemas, affect, and communication. In L. Donohew, H. E. Sypher, & E. T. Higgins (Eds.), *Communication, social cognition, and affect* (pp. 33–52). Hillsdale, NJ: Lawrence Erlbaum Associates.

Cronbach, L. J., Gleser, G. C., Nanda, H., & Rajaratnam, N. (1972). *The dependability of behavioral measurements: Theory of generalizability for scores and profiles.* New York: Wiley.

Culbertson, H. M. (1983). Three perspectives on American journalism. *Journalism Monographs, 83.*

Cunningham, A. (1999), Responsible advertisers: A contractualist approach to ethical power. *Journal of Mass Media Ethics, 14*(2), 82–94.

Cunningham, A., & Haley, E. (1998, August). *Preparing students for real-world ethical dilemmas: A stakeholder approach.* Paper presented to the Advertising Division of the Association for Education in Journalism and Mass Communication, Baltimore.

Davison, M. L., & Robbins, S. (1978). The reliability and validity of objective indices of moral development. *Applied Psychological Measurement, 2*(3), 391–403.

Deci, E. L., & Ryan, R. (1991). A motivational approach to self: Integration in personality. In R. A. Dienstbier (Ed.), *Nebraska Symposium on Motivation 1990: Perspectives on motivation* (pp. 237–288). Lincoln: University of Nebraska Press.

DePaulo, B. M., Kashy, D. A., Kirkendol, S. E., Wyer, M. M., & Epstein, J. A. (1996). Lying in everyday life. *Journal of Personality and Social Psychology, 70,* 979–995.

Devine, P. (1989). Stereotypes and prejudice: Their automatic and controlled components. *Journal of Personality and Social Psychology, 56*(1), 5–18.

Devine, P., & Monteith, M. J. (1999). Automaticity and control in stereotyping. In S. Chaiken & Y. Trope (Eds.), *Dual-process theories in social psychology* (pp. 339–360). New York: Guilford.

Doris, J. M. (2002). *Lack of character: Personality and moral behavior.* Cambridge, UK: Cambridge University Press.

Ekman, P. (2001). *Telling lies.* New York: Norton.

Elliot, D. (1989). Journalistic deception. In P. Y. Windt, P. C. Appleby, M. P. Battin, L. P. Francis, & B. M. Landesman (Eds.), *Ethical issues in the professions* (pp. 144–146). Englewood Cliffs, NJ: Prentice-Hall.

Elliot, D., & Culver, C. (1992). Defining and analyzing journalistic deception. *Journal of Mass Media Ethics, 7*(2), 69–84.

Ellis, A. (1986). Fanaticism that may lead to a nuclear holocaust: The contributions of scientific counseling and psychotherapy. *Journal of Counseling and Development, 65*(3), 146–151.

Entman, R. M. (1990). Modern racism and the images of blacks in local television news. *Critical Studies in Mass Communication, 7,* 332–345.

Entman, R. M. (1992). Blacks in the news: Television, modern racism and cultural change. *Journalism Quarterly, 69*(2), 341–361.

Entman, R. (1994). Representation and reality in the portrayal of blacks on network television news. *Journalism Quarterly, 71*(4), 509–520.

Erikson, E. H. (1964). *Childhood and society.* New York: Norton.

Ettema, J. S., & Glasser, T. L. (1998). *Custodians of conscience: Investigative journalism and public virtue.* New York: Columbia University Press.

Freid, C. (1978). *Right and wrong*. Cambridge, MA: Harvard University Press.

Gaertner, S., & McLaughlin, J. (1983). Racial stereotypes and ascriptions of positive and negative characteristics. *Social Psychology Quarterly, 46*(1), 23–30.

Garcia, M., & Stark, P. (1991). *Eyes on the news*. St. Petersburg, FL: Poynter Institute for Media Studies.

Gardner, H., Csikszentmihalyi, M., & Damon, W. (2001) *Good work: When excellence and ethics meet*. New York: Basic Books.

Gert, B. (1988). *Morality: A new justification of the moral rules*. New York: Oxford University Press.

Gibson, R., & Zillmann, D. (2000). Reading between the photographs: The influence of incidental pictoral information on issue perception. *Journalism & Mass Communication Quarterly, 77*(2), 355–366.

Gibson, R., Zillmann, D., & Sargent, S. (1999). Effects of photographs in news-magazine reports on issue perception. *Media Psychology, 1*(3), 207–228.

Gilliam, F. D., & Iyengar, S. (2000). Prime suspects: The influence of local television news on the viewing public. *American Journal of Political Science, 44*(3), 560.

Gilligan, C. (1982). *In a different voice: Psychological theory and women's development*. Cambridge, MA: Harvard University Press.

Glasser, T. L., & Ettema, J. S. (1989). Investigative journalism and the moral order. *Critical Studies in Mass Communication, 6*(1), 1–20.

Glock, C., & Stark, R. (1996). *Christian beliefs and anti-Semitism*. New York: Harper & Row.

Goldberg, V. (1991). *The power of photography: How photographs changed our lives*. New York: Abbeville.

Goodwin, G., & Smith, R. F. (1994). *Groping for ethics in journalism* (3rd ed.). Ames: Iowa State University Press.

Gould, S. J. (1981). *The mismeasure of man*. New York: Norton.

Graber, D. A. (1988). *Processing the news: How people tame the information tide* (2nd ed.). New York: Longman.

Graber, D. A. (1990). Seeing is remembering: How visuals contribute to learning from television news. *Journal of Communication, 40*, 134–155.

Grimes, T., & Drechsel, R. (1996). Word-picture juxtaposition, schemata, and defamation in television news. *Journalism & Mass Communication Quarterly, 73*(1), 169–180.

Habermas, J. (1989). *The structural transformation of the public sphere* (Thomas Burger, Trans.). Cambridge, MA: MIT Press.

Hacker, A. (1995). *Two nations: Black and white, separate, hostile and unequal* (2nd ed.). New York: Ballantine.

Hanson, G. (2002). Learning journalism ethics: The classroom versus the real world. *Journal of Mass Media Ethics, 17*(3), 235–247.

Harris, N. G. E. (1992). Codes of conduct for journalists. In A. Belsey & R. Chadwick (Eds.), *Ethical issues in journalism* (pp. 62–76). London: Routledge.

Harris, S., Mussen, P. H., & Rutherford, E. (1976). Some cognitive, behavioral, and personality correlates of maturity of moral judgment. *Journal of Genetic Psychology, 128*, 123–135.

Hodges, L. W. (1996). Ruminations about the communitarian debate, *Journal of Mass Media Ethics, 11*(3), 133–139.

Hoffman, J. K. (2000). *Empathy and moral development: Implications for caring and justice.* Cambridge, UK: Cambridge University Press.

Huh, H. L. (1994). The effect of newspaper picture size. *Visual Communication Quarterly, 1*(2), 14–15.

Hunt, S., & Chonko, L. (1987). Ethical problems of advertising agency executives. *Journal of Advertising, 6*(4), 16–24.

Husselbee, P., & Adams, A. (1996). Seeking instructional value: Publication of disturbing images in small community newspapers. *Newspaper Research Journal, 17*(3/4), 39–52.

Isen, A. M. (1984). Toward understanding the role of affect in cognition. In R. Wyer & T. Srull (Eds.), *Handbook of social cognition* (Vol. 3, pp. 179–236). Hillsdale, NJ: Lawrence Erlbaum Associates.

James, S. K. (1982). A study of ethical attitudes toward communicative acts in American society. (Doctoral dissertation, University of Kansas; 1982). *Dissertation Abstracts International, 43-09,* 2829.

Jhally, S. (Producer & Writer). (1998). *Advertising & the end of the world* [Video cassette]. Northampton, MA: Media Education Foundation.

Johnstone, J. W., Slawski, E. J., & Bowman, W. W. (1976). *The news people: A sociological portrait of American journalists and their work.* Urbana: University of Illinois Press.

Kane, M. (2002). Inferences about variance components and reliability-generalizability coefficients in the absence of random sampling. *Journal of Educational Measurement, 39*(2), 165–181.

Kant, I. (1785). *Groundwork on the metaphysics of morals.*

Keasey, C. B. (1971). Social participation as a factor in the moral development of preadolescents. *Developmental Psychology, 5,* 216–220.

Kieran, M. (1997). *Media ethics: A philosophical approach.* Westport, CT: Praeger.

Kirtley, J. (2000). Is it a crime? An overview of recent legal actions stemming from investigative reports. In M. Greenwald & J. Bernt (Eds.), *The big chill: Investigative reporting in the current media environment* (pp. 137–156). Ames: Iowa State University Press.

Kohlberg, L. (1958). *The development of modes of moral thinking and choice in the years 10 to 16.* Unpublished doctoral dissertation, University of Chicago.

Kohlberg, L. (1976). Moral stages and moralization. In T. Lichona (Ed.), *Moral development and behavior: Theory, research, and social issues* (pp. 163–185). New York: Holt, Rinehart, and Winston.

Kohlberg, L. (1981). *The philosophy of moral development: Moral stages and the idea of justice.* Cambridge, MA: Harper & Row.

Kohlberg, L. (1984). *The psychology of moral development: The nature and validity of moral stages.* San Francisco: Harper & Row.

Laitila, T. (1995). Journalistic codes of ethics in Europe. *European Journal of Communication, 10*(4), 513–526.

Lambeth, E. B. (1992). *Committed journalism: An ethic for the profession* (2nd ed.). Bloomington: Indiana University Press.

Langley, R. (1970). *Practical statistics simply explained.* New York: Dover.

Lawrence, J. A. (1978). *The component procedures of moral judgment-making.* Unpublished doctoral dissertation, University of Minnesota.

Lester, P. M. (1991). *Photojournalism: An ethical approach.* Hillsdale, NJ: Lawrence Erlbaum Associates.

Lester, P. M. (2000). *Visual communication: Images with messages.* Belmont, CA: Wadsworth/Thomson.

Levin, J. R., & Divine-Hawkins, P. (1974). Visual imagery as a prose-learning process. *Journal of Reading Behavior, 6,* 23–30.

Levin, J. R., & Mayer, R. E. (1993). Understanding illustrations in text. In B. K. Britton, A. Woodward, & M. Binkley (Eds.), *Learning from textbooks: Theory and practice* (pp. 95–113). Hillsdale, NJ: Lawrence Erlbaum Associates.

Levy, G. D. (2000). Individual differences in race schematicity as predictors of African American and White children's race-relevant memories and peer preferences. *The Journal of Genetic Psychology, 161*(4), 400–419.

Locke, D. C., & Tucker, D. O. (1988). Race and moral judgment development scores. *Counseling and Values, 32,* 232–235.

Luljak, T. (2000). The routine nature of journalistic deception. In D. Pritchard (Ed.), *Holding the media accountable: Citizens, ethics, and the law* (pp. 11–26). Bloomington: Indiana University Press.

Madigan, S. (1983). Picture memory. In J. C. Yuille (Ed.), *Imagery, memory and cognition: Essays in honor of Allan Paivio* (pp. 281–294). Hillsdale, NJ: Lawrence Erlbaum Associates.

Mandler, G. (1984). *Mind and body: The psychology of emotion and stress.* New York: Norton.

Martinson, D. (1996, August). *The ethical challenge for advertisers: To do the right, not "just" know it!* Paper presented to the Advertising Division of the Association for Education in Journalism and Mass Communication, Anaheim, CA.

McChesney, R. W. (1997). *Corporate media and the threat of democracy.* New York: Seven Stories Press.

McChesney, R. (1999). *Rich media, poor democracy.* Urbana: University of Illinois Press.

McCombs, M., Shaw, D. L., & Grey, D. (1976). *Handbook of reporting methods.* New York: Houghton Mifflin.

McNeel, S. P. (1994). College teaching and student moral development. In J. R. Rest & D. Narvaez (Eds.), *Moral development in the professions: Psychology and applied ethics* (pp. 27–49). Hillsdale, NJ: Lawrence Erlbaum Associates.

Merrill, J. C., & O'Dell, S. J. (1983). *Philosophy of journalism.* White Plains, NY: Longman.

Meyrowitz, J. (1985). *No sense of place: The impact of electronic media on social behavior.* New York: Oxford University Press.

Mieth, D. (1997). The basic norm of truthfulness: Its ethical justification and universality. In C. Christians & M. Traber (Eds.), *Communication ethics and universal values* (pp. 87–104). Thousand Oaks, CA: Sage.

Mill, J. S. (1859). *On liberty.*

Mill, J. S. (1861). *Utilitariansim.*

Newhagen, J. E., & Reeves, B. (1992). This evening's bad news: Effects of compelling television news images on memory. *Journal of Communication, 42,* 25–41.

Olasky, M. (1988). *The press and abortion, 1838–1988.* Hillsdale, NJ: Lawrence Erlbaum Associates.

Olejnik, A. B., & LaRue, A. A. (1980). Affect and moral reasoning. *Social Behavior & Personality: An International Journal, 8*(1), 75–79.

Oliver, M. B., & Fonash, D. (2002). Race and crime in the news: Whites' identification and misidentification of violent and nonviolent criminal suspects. *Media Psychology, 4*(2), 137–156.

Paivio, A. (1983). The empirical case for dual coding. In J. C. Yuille (Ed.), *Imagery, memory and cognition* (pp. 307–332). Hillsdale, NJ: Lawrence Erlbaum Associates.

Paivio, A. (1986). *Mental representations: A dual coding approach.* New York: Oxford University Press.

Park, H., Weigold, M., & Treise, D. (1999), Advertising ethics: South Korean and American perceptions and ideology. *Journal of Mass Media Ethics, 14*(2), 95–106.

Parker, R. J. (1990). The relationship between dogmatism, orthodox Christian beliefs, and ethical judgment. *Counseling and Values, 34*(3), 213–216.

Paterno, S. (1997, May). The lying game. *American Journalism Review,* pp. 40–45.

Patterson, M. J., & Hall, M. W. (1998). Abortion, moral maturity and civic journalism. *Critical Studies in Mass Communication, 15*(2), 91–115.

Perry, W. O. (1968). *Intellectual development in the college years: A scheme.* New York: Holt, Rinehart and Winston.

Peters, J. D., & Cmiel, K. (1989). Democracy and American mass communication theory: Dewey, Lippmann, Lazarsfeld. *Communication, 11*(3), 199–220.

Petty, R. E., & Cacioppo, J. T. (1986). *Communication and persuasion: Central and peripheral routes to attitude change.* New York: Springer-Verlag.

Petty, R. E., Cacioppo, J. T., & Goldman, R. (1981). Personal involvement as a determinant of argument-based persuasion. *Journal of Personality and Social Psychology, 41*(5), 847–855.

Piaget, J. (1965). *The moral judgment of the child.* New York: Free Press. (Original work published 1932)

Poindexter, P. M., & Stroman, C. (1981). Blacks and television: A review of the research literature. *Journal of Broadcasting & Electronic Media, 25*(2), 103–122.

Ponemon, L. (1992). Auditor underreporting of time and moral reasoning: An experimental lab study. *Contemporary Accounting Research, 9,* 171–189.

Ponemon, L. (1993), The influence of ethical reasoning on auditors' perceptions of management's competence and integrity. *Advances in Accounting, 11,* 1–29.

Power, S. (2002). *The problem from hell. America in the age of genocide.* New York: Basic Books.

Price, R. D. (1973). Situational determinants of ethical judgments (Doctoral dissertation, Ohio University, 1973). *Dissertation Abstracts, 33-11,* 5547.

Pryluck, C. (1976). *Sources of meaning in motion pictures and television.* New York: Arno.

Rawls, J. (1971). *A theory of justice.* Cambridge, MA: Harvard University Press.

Reeves, J. L., & Campbell, R. (1994). *Cracked coverage: Television news, the anti-drug crusade, and the Reagan legacy.* Durham, NC: Duke University Press.

Reid, H. G., & Yanarella, E. J. (1980). The tyranny of the catagorical: Of Kohlberg and the politics of moral development. In R. Wilson & G. J. Schochet (Eds.), *Moral development and politics* (pp. 107–129). New York: Praeger.

Rest, J. R. (1979). *Development in judging moral issues.* Minneapolis: University of Minnesota Press.

Rest, J. R. (1983). Morality. In P. H. Mussen (Ed.), *Handbook of child psychology, Vol. III cognitive development* (pp. 556–629), New York: Wiley.

Rest, J. R. (1986). *Moral development: Advances in research and theory.* New York: Praeger.

Rest, J. R. (1993). Research on moral judgment in college students. In A. Garrod (Ed.), *Approaches to moral development: New research and emerging themes* (pp. 176–195). New York: Teacher's College Press.

Rest, J. R., & Narvaez, D. (1984). *Supplement to guide for DIT-1.* Minneapolis: Center for the Study of Ethical Development, University of Minnesota.

Rest, J. R., Narvaez, D., Bebeau, M. J., & Thoma, S. J. (1999). *Postconventional moral thinking: A neo-Kohlbergian approach.* Mahwah, NJ: Lawrence Erlbaum Associates.

Richards, E. (1994). *Cocaine true, cocaine blue.* New York: Aperture.

Riffe, D., Lacy, S., & Fico, F. G. (1998). *Analyzing media messages: Using quantitative content analysis in research.* Mahwah, NJ: Lawrence Erlbaum Associates.

Ross, W. D. (1930). *The right and the good.* Oxford, UK: Clarendon Press.

Singletary, M. W., Caudill, S., Caudill, E., & White, A. (1990). Motives for ethical decision-making. *Journalism Quarterly, 67*(4), 964–972.

Sontag, S. (1977). *On photography.* New York: Anchor.

Stocking, S. H., & Gross, P. H. (1989). *How do journalists think: A proposal for the study of cognitive bias in newsmaking.* Bloomington: ERIC Clearinghouse on Reading and Communication Skills, Smith Research Center, Indiana University.

Teal, E. J., & Carroll, A. B. (1999). Moral reasoning skills: Are entrepreneurs different? *Journal of Business Ethics, 19*(3), 229–240.

Thoma, S. (1986). Estimating gender differences in the comprehension and preference of moral issues. *Developmental Review, 6,* 165–180.

Thorne, L. (2000). The development of two measures to assess accountants' prescriptive and deliberative moral reasoning. *Behavioral Research in Accounting, 12,* 139–169.

Tucker, E., & Stout, D. (1999). The moral development of educators. *Journal of Mass Media Ethics, 14*(2), 107–118.

Turner, R. E., Edgley, C., & Olmstead, F. (1975, Spring). Information control in conversations: Honesty is not always the best policy. *Kansas Journal of Sociology*, pp. 68–71.

Valenti, J. M. (1998). Ethical decision making in environmental communication. *Journal of Mass Media Ethics, 13*(4), 219–231.

Valentino, N. A. (1999). Crime news and the priming of racial attitudes during evaluations of the presidency. *Public Opinion Quarterly, 63*(Fall), 293–230.

Voakes, P. S. (1997). Public perceptions of journalists' ethical motivations. *Journalism & Mass Communication Quarterly, 74*(1), 23–38.

Voakes, P. S. (1998). What were you thinking? A survey of journalists who were sued for invasion of privacy. *Journalism & Mass Communication Quarterly, 75*(2), 378–393.

Waisbord, S. R. (1996). Investigative journalism and political accountability in South American democracies. *Critical Studies in Mass Communication, 13*, 343–363.

Wanta, W. (1988). The effects of dominant photographs: An agenda-setting experiment. *Journalism Quarterly, 65*, 107–111.

Weaver, D., Beam, R., Brownlee, B., Voakes, P., & Wilhoit, G. C. (in press). *The American journalist in the 21st century.* Mahwah, NJ: Lawrence Erlbaum Associates.

Weaver, D. H., & Wilhoit, G. C. (1986). *The American journalist: A portrait of U.S. news people and their work.* Bloomington: Indiana University Press.

Weaver, D. H., & Wilhoit, G. C. (1996). *The American journalist in the 1990s: U.S. news people at the end of an era.* Mahwah, NJ: Lawrence Erlbaum Associates.

Weinberg, S. (1997). Undercover investigations. In E. D. Cohen & D. Elliot (Eds.), *Journalism ethics: A handbook* (pp. 107–109). Santa Barbara, CA: ABC-CLIO.

Westbrook, T. L. (1995). The cognitive moral development of journalists: Distribution and implications for news production. (Doctoral dissertation, University of Texas at Austin, 1995). *Dissertation Abstracts International, 56*(3-A).

White, C., Bushnell, N., & Regnemer, I. (1978). Moral development in Bahamian school children: A three-year examination of Kohlberg's stages of moral development. *Developmental Psychology, 14*(1), 58–65.

White, H. A., & Pearce, R. C. (1991). Validating an ethical motivations scale: Convergence and predictive ability. *Journalism & Mass Communication Quarterly, 68*(3), 455–464.

White, H. A., & Singletary, M. W. (1993). Internal work motivation: Predictor of using ethical heuristics and motivations. *Journalism & Mass Communication Quarterly, 70*(2), 381–392.

Whitlow, S. S., & Van Tubergen, G. N. (1978). Patterns of ethical decisions among investigative reporters. *Mass Communication Review, 6*(1), 2–9.

Winch, S. (2000). In M. Greenwald & J. Bernt (Eds.), *The big chill: Investigative reporting in the current media environment* (pp. 121–136). Ames: Iowa State University Press.

Wulfemeyer, K. (1990). Defining ethics in electronic journalism: Perceptions of news directors. *Journalism Quarterly, 67*, 984–991.

Author Index

Subject Index